# Ethics for Anthropological Research and Practice

## Linda M. Whiteford
*University of South Florida*

## Robert T. Trotter II
*Northern Arizona University*

WAVELAND

PRESS, INC.

Long Grove, Illinois

*This book is dedicated to our students,*
*fellow researchers, teachers, and practitioners,*
*and to our spouses who have supported our careers*
*in many ways for many years. Thanks.*
*— LMW and RTT*

For information about this book, contact:
Waveland Press, Inc.
4180 IL Route 83, Suite 101
Long Grove, IL  60047-9580
(847) 634-0081
info@waveland.com
www.waveland.com

# Contents

# Preface

Anthropologists face many dilemmas about how to ethically conduct their research and practice in complicated, crosscultural environments. In this book, we provide some guidelines by which to think about the ethical practice of anthropology in community, organizational, or clinical settings. Many of the viewpoints presented are based on U.S. and European laws, treaties, and practice. Since the creation of the internationally based Nuremberg Code and the domestically based Belmont Report, United States and other Western-dominated cultures have increasingly codified ways to control research on human subjects and have pushed for a universal code that is acceptable to those cultures.

We also present alternative or competing viewpoints about the ethics of anthropological research and practice. While both the Nuremberg Code and The Belmont Report (and many of the laws that followed) were generated by ethical failures in the practice of biomedicine, social science research and practice has not been without its own lapses in ethics that put participants at risk and have resulted in further codes and restrictions on anthropological research.

We teach in anthropology departments where both undergraduate and graduate courses are offered in ethics and anthropology. Our decision to write this book came, in part, from our students who wanted a resource book on ethics and anthropology for their own reference and future work within the field. It is not designed to duplicate existing books but rather to provide a brief review of the history of ethics in the discipline of anthropology, an identification of basic principles critical to the ethical practice of anthropology, the provision of a selected number of professional codes, two schematics for systematic ethical decision making, and five cases that are useful for problem solving.

It is hoped that this brief guide for current and future anthropologists will prompt discussions of how to practice anthropology ethically. In the book, we focus on concepts that shape our own work and that of our students and colleagues—respect for persons, beneficence, and justice—and that are part of the larger international discussion and practice of ethics. In writing this book, we had in mind our students who may become teachers, researchers, practitioners but will always be anthropologists, and we tried to suggest the ways in which a conscious approach to ethics in the design and conduct of anthropological research and practice can be rewarding.

Each of the topics we present could be expanded on and discussed in much greater detail with many more references and examples. Luckily, there are other books on anthropology and ethics that do just that, and hopefully, we have referenced them here. Many of the examples we have included come from our own experiences and our own readings and, thus, reflect our own interests. Both of us are medical anthropologists, and while many of the examples in this text may reflect that bias, we believe that the substantive content of the book makes it appropriate for all anthropologists and other social scientists who engage in research and practice and wish to do so ethically.

## ACKNOWLEDGEMENTS

As with most projects, this one was a long time in coming. Both coauthors had been teaching ethics in their universities (Whiteford as a required course for the graduate program at the University of South Florida, and Trotter similarly but at Northern Arizona University). Kate Brelsford first took Trotter's course as an MA student at NAU, and then she took Whiteford's course as a PhD student at USF. It is she who first suggested that we write this book together. And, in the true style of collaborative teaching, we asked her to help us by creating a series of exercises that students could use to learn about ethics in anthropological research and practice.

Whiteford then modified those original ideas and shared them with the class she was teaching. As a result, the ethical dilemma cases included in this book come from both Kate and the students in Whiteford's 2007 ethics class at USF. So, we thank Kate for her original idea, encouragement, and help, as well as thanking all the students from those classes we both taught, who helped us refine the ethical problem-solving guide and the ethical dilemmas.

In addition, our appreciation is extended to the two reviewers who provided constructive and insightful comments to improve our original draft, and to Cecilia Vindrola who struggled to complete the references.

*Chapter One*

# The Complex Nature
# of Ethics

In our daily lives we are beset by choices, quandaries, and dilemmas. We resolve them by seeking guidance from a variety of sources, such as our own norms and traditions, religious doctrine, and legal codes. We also resolve them based on the situations in which they occur, guided by our own personal morals and beliefs. People who are members of a profession, such as anthropology, often rely on disciplinary codes of conduct, standards for professional behavior, and other codifications of ethics to help them address the quandaries and dilemmas they face in their professional lives.

Most professional associations have guidelines, for professional behavior. Since anthropology has five recognized subdivisions (cultural, linguistics, archaeology, physical, and applied), there are multiple ethical guidelines and several principles of professional ethics that may apply at the same time for an anthropologist, depending on the research focus, the applied projects, and even the teaching activities. Some of these established ethical standards have been published by the American Anthropological Association (AAA), the National Association for the Practice of Anthropology (NAPA), the Society for Applied Anthropology (SfAA), the Society for American Archaeology (SAA), the American Association of Physical Anthropologists (AAPA), and the World Archaeological Congress (WAC). These ethical guidelines cover anthropological research, teaching, and practice (praxis) while also focusing on the particular ethical dilemmas that challenge each of the subfields. The ethical principles, guidelines and rules of each subdiscipline have many elements in common as well as ones that are highly specific to that endeavor.

1

This book focuses predominately on the ethical guidelines that steer sociocultural research and the eventual application of that research to living human groups. That is not to say, however, that the ethical principles and practices discussed do not also apply to linguistic anthropology, archeology, and physical anthropology in the cases where they deal with living humans, as well as to the other social sciences (psychology, political science, sociology, economics, educational research) and to all of the human research sciences in general.

In anthropological literature, via the Internet, and at professional meetings, anthropologists have maintained lively debates and engaged in critical and reflective dialogues about the role of ethics in anthropology. Part of that dialogue explores the issue of how do we identify individuals or projects that have violated the profession's ethical principles (or more global ethical conditions) and what should we, as anthropologists, do about those ethical lapses? Part of the dialogue has been cautionary or prescriptive and has presented situations that anthropologists should avoid or ways in which they should behave in their professional lives. Part of the dialogue has also been about what role professional anthropological associations should have in both policing their members' activities and publicly identifying and sanctioning ethical failures.

Some professional associations have decided to sanction (publicly identify, expel, or disavow) members who have broken ethical rules of behavior. Others have sanctioned their members for raising politically uncomfortable issues. As an example, in 1919 Franz Boas, writing in the magazine *The Nation*, denounced anthropologists who acted as spies in World War I. What were the consequences of this denouncement? At the December 30, 1919, meeting of the American Anthropological Association in Cambridge, Boas was censured, stripped of his membership in the association's governing council, and forced to resign his position on the National Security Council and resign from the association. What rule did Boas break? He had written a public and vigorous protest against scientists (specifically anthropologists) who used the cloak of science to misrepresent their actions. In his letter published in *The Nation*, Boas wrote: "In consequence of their acts every nation will look with distrust upon the visiting foreign investigator who wants to do honest work, suspecting sinister designs. Such action has raised a new barrier against the development of international friendly cooperation" (Boas 1919). Boas sounded the alarm in 1919. Since then, the discipline has struggled with the role of anthropologists and the use (or misuse) of anthropology in wars, armed conflicts, military actions, and proposed counterinsurgency projects.

Some professional associations, such as the American Medical Association, require their members to be certified or licensed to reinforce members' adherence to ethical guidelines for professional behavior. If the public or other members of the professional association find that a member has breached the ethical guidelines, the association can revoke his or her license or certificate. Other associations have no way to sanction members for not following professional codes of conduct other than through public notice, censure, or revocation of membership. The discipline of anthropology has neither a certification process nor the authority or means to enforce adherence to the various ethical codes and guidelines across the discipline. This means that it is up to individuals, as well as collectives of anthropologists, to encourage ethical behavior on the part of practitioners, researchers, and/or educators. Some, but not all, postgraduate educational programs in anthropology include courses on ethics, but students not yet at that level of education may lack an understanding of the ethical guidelines and practices within the discipline, how they originated, and why they are useful tools. This book fills this knowledge gap.

## ANTHROPOLOGY AND ETHICAL CHALLENGES

Anthropologists face ethical challenges on many levels, including before, during, and after their research is conducted, as well as when conducting professional activities such as teaching, applied practice, and knowledge dissemination within and across competing social and cultural boundaries. We feel anthropologists must be particularly ethically vigilant when they use anthropological theory, knowledge, or praxis when working with vulnerable populations, that is, people who, due to their circumstances, have less ability to make decisions, speak for themselves, or protect their own interests. The types of circumstances that contribute to vulnerability include, but are not limited to, financial instability, place of residence, age, illness or disability, and lack of communication skills. The history of human research is littered with the cultural debris of harmful actions on the part of researchers and their sponsors. Principles, guidelines and laws that protect people from unethical research have been established throughout the world, and following them is a critical, ethical—yet often challenging— requirement for conducting research on human subjects and protecting them from harm at the hands of researchers.

## HISTORY OF ETHICAL PRINCIPLES
## AND GUIDELINES IN ANTHROPOLOGY

Anthropologists have been intimately involved in the public debates and explorations of the ethics of research ever since the emer-

gence of the discipline in the late 1800s, when much of the ethical elements of the debate revolved around the meaning of evolution, the
relationship of science to theology, and the nature of "civilization" with
regard to other forms of social complexity, as opposed to other cultural
conditions. Since that time, the discussion of ethics in anthropology
has consistently paralleled the concerns, explorations, and debates
focused on science in general, on the effects of technology and globalization on all cultures around the world, on war and conflict, and on
the emerging ethical concerns in the other social sciences. However,
because of the anthropological principle of *cultural relativism* (describing cultures from their own point of view rather than relying solely on
an outsider's view of them) and the importance of avoiding *ethnocentrism* (the perspective that one's own group is superior to others) in
sociocultural anthropology, the anthropological debate on ethics often
goes in a different direction, for at least some of the ethical issues and
principles, from the ethical debates in other disciplines. This is especially true when debates focus on the differences between the cultural
values of Western civilization and those of non-Western cultures, or
between the developed world and the developing world. Carole Nagengast (2004), among others, has written extensively about the struggle
that anthropologists have in trying to reconcile the principle of cultural relativism with concepts such as universal human rights (for
example, a North American anthropologist conducting participant
observation research among members of a cultural group whose
behaviors are guided by principles that are humane and acceptable to
them [cultural relativism] but are not so by Western standards [uni-
versal human rights]).

The following time line presents key points in the ethical evolution of anthropological guidelines for research and practice:

> 1947–48 American Anthropological Association (AAA) Position on
>    Declaration of Human Rights
> 1949 Society for Applied Anthropology Professional Code of Ethics
> 1967 AAA Revised Statement on Ethics
> 1971 AAA Formal Rules of Ethics
> 1986 AAA Principles of Professional Responsibility
> 1987 National Association for the Practice of Anthropology Ethical
>    Guidelines
> 1990 Revision of AAA Principles of Professional Responsibility
> 1995 Report of AAA Ethics Commission
> 1998 AAA Code of Ethics

One of the early public explorations of ethics in anthropological
research was the AAA's participation in the drafting of the Universal
Declaration of Human Rights (UDHR) (Nagengast 2004). One of the
key anthropological contributions to the declaration was the establishment of the principle of cultural relativism (Herskovits 1958). As

Nagengast (2004) pointed out, this concern with the importance of embracing cultural relativity was the reason that, in 1947, the American Anthropological Association initially opposed the UDHR, which made eligibility for basic human rights expansive and inclusive:

> The following basic premises underlie the UDHR: (a) people do not have to do or be anything in particular in order to enjoy human rights, and rights are extended equally to all people everywhere by virtue of shared humanity; they are, in other words, rights rather than entitlements; (b) the state is responsible for both ensuring and defending the rights of all people and people within its borders; and (c) a higher international order supersedes the national state. (Nagengast 2004:110–111)

How could the professional association representing a discipline that is dependent on the good will of people to participate in its research and that has a history of studying vulnerable populations refuse to support such a declaration? This opposition from the AAA is difficult to reconcile with the aims of the declaration that were directed at the protection of "free speech, assembly, religion, and basic necessities like food, health care, and housing: the right to work and to equal and fair pay for equal work: and freedom from slavery, torture, and cruel, inhuman, and degrading treatment" (Nagengast 2004:110).

The first formal code of ethics for anthropologists was published by the Society for Applied Anthropology in 1949. This code was publicly discussed and was soon followed by written statements from prominent members of the American Anthropological Association. Some of the key ethical debates among anthropologists occurred along with other public debates about the increasing threat of nuclear war, the Korean and Vietnam wars, and the civil rights movements in the United States and in many other nations. The original SfAA guidelines (1949) were revised several times, including the 1967 Revised Statement on Ethics, and the 1971 Formal Rules adopted by the American Anthropological Association, both of which were strongly impacted by the unethical use of anthropological research and findings during the Vietnam War and in cold war conflicts played out in Latin America. Questions of research ethics came back to the discipline in a very public way with the publication of Patrick Tierney's *Darkness in El Dorado: How Scientists and Journalists Devastated the Amazon* (2000), a journalistic account of research malfeasance in the Amazon. While many of the author's claims, for instance, that a measles epidemic was purposefully introduced into the Yanomami in order to watch its course, were proven to be inaccurate, there were underlying truths in the exposé that were both disturbing and provocative, creating a new generation of discussions about ethics and the discipline of anthropology. The guidelines for ethical anthropological research were subsequently reviewed and revised to take into account more recent changes in the standards and practices that are the core of anthropological research (AAA 2005).

It is vitally important for anthropologists to be familiar with their professional ethical obligations, as well as with national and international ethical principles, rules, regulations, and discussions. The following statements are excerpts from the AAA Principles of Professional Responsibility (http://www.aaanet.org/stmts/ethstmnt.htm). Adopted in 1986, it has been discussed and debated on virtually a yearly basis since that time. The excerpts provide a framework for both understanding and professionally applying the formal principles and rules of ethics that are discussed in detail in the chapters that follow. A more extensive discussion of the development of ethical guidelines in the history of anthropology is also available in works by Carolyn Fluehr-Lobban (2003).

### Excerpts from AAA's Principles of Professional Responsibility

In a field of such complex involvements, misunderstandings, conflicts, and the necessity to make choices among conflicting values are bound to arise and to generate ethical dilemmas. . . . Where these conditions cannot be met, the anthropologist would be well-advised not to pursue the particular piece of research.

**1. Relations with those studied.** In research, anthropologists' paramount responsibility is to those they study. When there is a conflict of interest, these individuals must come first. Anthropologists must do everything in their power to protect the physical, social, and psychological welfare and to honor the dignity and privacy of those studied.

**2. Responsibility to the public.** Anthropologists are also responsible to the public—all presumed consumers of their professional efforts.

**3. Responsibility to the discipline.** Anthropologists bear responsibility for the good reputation of the discipline and its practitioners.

**4. Responsibility to students.** In relations with students, anthropologists should be candid, fair, nonexploitative, and committed to the student's welfare and progress.

**5. Responsibility to sponsors.** In relations with sponsors of research, anthropologists should be honest about their qualifications, capabilities, aims. . . . Anthropologists should be especially careful not to promise or imply acceptance of conditions contrary to their professional ethics or competing commitments. . . . Anthropologists must retain the right to make all ethical decisions in their research.

**6. Responsibilities to one's own government and to host governments.** In relation with their own government and with host governments, research anthropologists should . . . demand assurance that they will not be required to compromise their professional responsibilities and ethics as a condition of their permission to pursue research.

**Epilogue.** When anthropologists, by their actions, jeopardize peoples studied, professional colleagues, students or others, or if they otherwise betray their professional commitments, their colleagues may legitimately inquire into the propriety of those actions, and take such measures as lie within the legitimate powers of their Association as the membership of the Association deems appropriate.

These statements are generally accepted by anthropologists, but not without debate, discussion, challenges, and recommendations for revision to make these guidelines more (or less) compatible with both national and international formal ethical principles and guidelines. The AAA Committee on Ethics has advanced the discussions of the guidelines through public forums, the publication of provocative case studies, and columns in the *Anthropology Newsletter*, since the time these guidelines were formally adopted and reviewed. In part, those discussions have revolved around changes in anthropological theory, as well as methodological advances in qualitative studies, combined with the impact of technology (virtual communities and communication). One of the critical trends in the anthropological ethics debate is the ongoing tension in anthropology between science and humanism, between positivism and other more interpretive paradigms, and between modernism (especially the concept of progress and the concept of universalism) and postmodernism (especially the concepts of cultural particularism, cultural relativism, and constant cultural constructionism). Furthermore, members of the AAA Committee on Ethics have provided an important counterpoint to the tendency of anthropologists to rely on individual ethics and on taking a situational ethical stance. Basically, situational ethics is a system of ethics by which acts are judged within their contexts instead of by categorical principles. This definition is often extended to maintain that situational ethics are ethical decisions or ethical judgments that are made on the basis of an individual's moral or amoral viewpoint at a particular place and time, instead of judgments that are made from the basis of accepted principles or guidelines. AAA members pointed out that situational ethics all too often evolves into a case of "the end justifies the means," while also acknowledging the complexity of these issues.

> Our goal is to change the attitude that ethical behavior is rooted in good intentions alone. This broader and more complex view takes into consideration cultural context, relevant history, and emerging interdisciplinary and international norms of behavior regarding ethical decision making that are entwined with research involving humans. Moreover, the AAA needs to work with specialists in var-

ious subfields to make them more aware of their existing statements on ethics as well as the limitations of the current AAA Code
of Ethics. (Pyburn and Fluehr-Lobban 2006:21)

Anthropological ethicists have also been actively challenging
anthropologists to take charge of their own code of ethics and to be
proactive in both promulgating and supporting that code, because

> if we are, indeed, unable or unwilling to make statements about
> the ethical values of our profession, and how they are conceptual-
> ized and practiced by anthropologists in dynamic contexts, then
> we leave the interpretation of our ethics and principles of profes-
> sionalism to the courts, to journalists or others to determine them
> or shape them through their institutions. We also abdicate a fun-
> damental responsibility of a professional association and its lead-
> ership. (Fluehr-Lobban 2006b:5)

The guide to ethical behavior from the Society for Applied
Anthropology (n.d.) provides an additional view of how anthropologists have attempted to operationalize abstract concepts and make
them concrete so that they can be applied in both research and practice (http://www.sfaa.net/sfaaethic.html).

### SfAA Ethical and Professional Responsibilities

This statement is a guide to professional behavior for the members of the Society for Applied Anthropology. As members or fel-
lows of the society, we shall act in ways consistent with the
responsibilities stated below irrespective of the specific circumstances of our employment.

1. To the peoples we study we owe disclosure of our research goals,
methods, and sponsorship. The participation of people in our
research activities shall only be on a voluntary basis. We shall provide a means through our research activities and in subsequent
publications to maintain the confidentiality of those we study. The
peoples we study must be made aware of the likely limits of confidentiality and must not be promised a greater degree of confidentiality than can be realistically expected under current legal
circumstances in our respective nations. We shall, within the limits of our knowledge, disclose any significant risks to those we
study that may result from our activities.

2. To the communities ultimately affected by our activities we owe
respect for their dignity, integrity, and worth. We recognize that
human survival is contingent upon the continued existence of a diversity of human communities, and guide our professional activities
accordingly. We will avoid taking or recommending action on behalf
of a sponsor which is harmful to the interests of the community.

3. To our social colleagues we have the responsibility to not engage
in actions that impede their reasonable professional activities.
Among other things, this means that, while respecting the needs,

responsibilities, and legitimate proprietary interests of our sponsors we should not impede the flow of information about research outcomes and professional practice techniques. We shall accurately report the contributions of colleagues to our work. We shall not condone falsification or distortion by others. We should not prejudice communities or agencies against a colleague for reasons of personal gain.

4. To our students, interns, or trainees, we owe nondiscriminatory access to our training services. We shall provide training which is informed, accurate, and relevant to the needs of the larger society. We recognize the need for continuing education so as to maintain our skill and knowledge at a high level. Our training should inform students as to their ethical responsibilities. Student contributions to our professional activities, including both research and publication, should be adequately recognized.

5. To our employers and other sponsors we owe accurate reporting of our qualifications and competent, efficient, and timely performance of the work we undertake for them. We shall establish a clear understanding with each employer or other sponsor as to the nature of our professional responsibilities. We shall report our research and other activities accurately. We have the obligation to attempt to prevent distortion or suppression of research results or policy recommendations by concerned agencies.

6. To society as a whole we owe the benefit of our special knowledge and skills in interpreting sociocultural systems. We should communicate our understanding of human life to the society at large.

When ethics is expanded to include anthropological and other social science research and practice outside the United States, there is increasingly intensive international and crosscultural scrutiny of what anthropologists do and how ethically they do it. One trend in the globalization of ethics is the creation of international guidelines for sociocultural research (Macer n.d.) that take into account crosscultural variations in ethical principles and processes. One example of this movement is the development of the Ethical Guidelines for Social Science Research in Health (NCESSRH n.d.) by the National Committee for Ethics in Social Science Research in Health in New Delhi, India. The following excerpt establishes the primary principles that frame this approach to international ethical guidelines for the social sciences (http://www.hsph.harvard.edu/bioethics/guidelines/ethical.html).

### Ethical Guidelines for Social Science Research in Health
#### Section II
#### Ethical Principles for Research
II. 1. Four well-known moral principles constitute the basis for ethics in research. They are:

(i) *The Principle of Non-maleficence:* Research must not cause harm to the participants in particular and to people in general.

*(ii) The Principle of Beneficence:* Research should also make a positive contribution towards the welfare of people.

*(iii) The Principle of Autonomy:* Research must respect and protect the rights and dignity of participants.

*(iv) The Principle of Justice:* The benefits and risks of research should be fairly distributed among people.

II. 2. Ten general ethical principles, presently relevant for social science research in health in India, are as follows:

*(i) Essentiality:* For undertaking research it is necessary to make all possible efforts to get and give adequate consideration to existing literature/knowledge and its relevance, and the alternatives available on the subject/issue under the study.

*(ii) Maximisation of public interest and of social justice:* Research is a social activity, carried out for the benefit of society. It should be undertaken with the motive of maximization of public interest and social justice.

*(iii) Knowledge, ability and commitment to do research:* Sincere commitment to research in general and to the relevant subject in particular, and readiness to acquire adequate knowledge, ability and skill for undertaking particular research are essential prerequisites for good and ethical research.

*(iv) Respect and protection of autonomy, rights and dignity of participants:* Research involving participation of individual(s) must not only respect, but also protect the autonomy, the rights and the dignity of participants. The participation of individual(s) must be voluntary and based on informed consent.

*(v) Privacy, anonymity and confidentiality:* All information and records provided by participants or obtained directly or indirectly on/about the participants are confidential. For revealing or sharing any information that may identify participants, permission of the participants is essential.

*(vi) Precaution and risk minimisation:* All research carries some risk to the participants and to society. Taking adequate precautions and minimising and mitigating risks is, therefore, essential.

*(vii) Non-exploitation*: Research must not unnecessarily consume the time of participants or make them incur undue loss of resources and income. It should not expose them to risks due to participation in the research. The relationship within the research team, including student and junior members, should be based on the principle of non-exploitation. Contribution of each member of the research team should be properly acknowledged and recognised.

*(viii) Public domain:* All persons and organisations connected to research should make adequate efforts to make public in appropriate manner and form, and at appropriate time, information on the research undertaken, and the relevant results and implications of completed research.

*(ix) Accountability and transparency:* The conduct of research must be fair, honest and transparent. It is desirable that institutions and researchers are amenable to social and financial review

of their research by an appropriate and responsible social body. They should also make appropriate arrangements for the preservation of research records for a reasonable period of time.

*(x) Totality of responsibility:* The responsibility for due observance of all principles of ethics and guidelines devolves on all those directly or indirectly connected with the research. They include institution(s) where the research is conducted, researcher(s), sponsors/funders and those who publish material generated from research.

The AAA and the SfAA guidelines focus on the anthropologist's responsibility to his or her research subjects, sponsors, students, colleagues, and the discipline as a whole, while the NCESSRH guidelines provide a set of principles for rules-based conduct from the community perspective. It is also valuable to note that the AAA statement includes a paragraph on the anthropologist's responsibility to one's own and host governments, while the SfAA guide includes an explicit statement about full disclosure to the community being studied of research goals, objectives, and methods to be employed, which are concepts that take on added meaning in light of the long tradition of abuse of trust identified by Boas in 1919 and continuing well into the twenty-first century.

The NCESSRH guidelines clearly take into account the primary ethical principles that are the foundation for the American Anthropological Association, the SfAA guidelines, and the formal research ethics guidelines followed in the United States and by international treaties worldwide (see chapters 3, 4, and 5 for a detailed explanation of these principles). At the same time, these principles add a number of the sociocultural concerns addressed in the social science research literature and the ethical guidelines for many professional social science organizations (Van den Hoonaard 2002; Washburn 1998; Zechenter 1997). Many people feel social science research, in general, and ethnographic (anthropological) research, in particular, are significantly threatened by the application of a rules-based set of regulations on human research, as opposed to a contextual and situationally based set of regulations (Bourgois 1990; Fluehr-Lobban 1994; Sieber, Plattner, Rubin 2002). The thought questions and the ethical dilemma cases presented in this book are designed to allow readers to explore and address these conditions from both a principle-based and a more existential- or postmodernist-based foundation in anthropological ethics.

## APPLYING ETHICAL DECISION MAKING TO REAL-LIFE PROBLEMS

One challenge anthropologists face is to construct and conduct their research in an ethical manner, based on their own culture's prin-

ciples and guidelines for ethical research, while remaining true to the
relevant principles and guidelines of the culture they are studying.
They have to successfully anticipate, address, and appropriately apply
the numerous, often vague, sometimes culture-bound, and challenging
national and international rules, guidelines, and treaty obligations on
the ethical conduct of science and research (Fluehr-Lobban 2006a;
Marshall 2003; Marshall and Daar 2000; Nagengast 2004). A second
complementary challenge is for anthropologists to conduct their nonresearch professional activities ethically as well (Marshall 1992).
Anthropologists should behave in an ethical manner with colleagues,
communities, and those who seek their knowledge and advice. They
must be particularly vigilant when they use anthropological theory,
knowledge, or praxis that might cause direct (and sometimes indirect)
harm to vulnerable people.

This book addresses both ethical dilemmas and ethical failures,
but the ethical dilemmas are more common in most anthropologists'
lives and are also frequently more amenable to both prevention and
intervention efforts. Ethical dilemmas are different from simple ethical failures. There is a clear *ethical failure* any time a researcher
coerces individuals to participate in the research, lies or deceives in
the informed consent process, hides or misrepresents project-related
risks, puts a community at risk, or conducts research that will not
benefit the people involved in the research. Professional guidelines
exist specifically to prevent intentional types of ethical failures (cf.
AAA 1986; SfAA n.d.).

A large number of ethical problems for anthropologists result
from the unanticipated consequences of a research design, from conflicts among stakeholders (participants in and beneficiaries of the
research), or from an *ethical dilemma*—a particular problem that
involves the clash of two positive ethical principles, and when adherence to one of the principles may violate another. For example, your
research subjects may have been promised confidentiality for any
information they provide (such as their health status), but they may
also have been promised that no harm will come to them as a part of
the research. A clear conflict between the principles of confidentiality
and do no harm exists if a married couple is enrolled in an AIDS
project, and the research uncovers that one partner is HIV-positive,
and the infected person is having unprotected sex with his or her
uninfected partner but is not telling the partner about being HIV-positive. In this kind of situation, the researcher may have to decide if he
or she has a greater obligation to protect confidentiality or to prevent
harm to the uninfected person. Preventing harm may help the one
individual, but breaking confidentiality may harm the entire project,
since anyone who hears about the breach might either quit the project
or not participate.

There are times when the researcher is forced to decide which of two ethical principles takes precedence in a particular research situation, and the choice of one principle causes the other principle to be violated in some minor or major way. Either way, it is a dilemma, and the resolution will depend on a series of decisions the anthropologist must make that bears in mind principles and guidelines of a professional ethical statement, alongside his or her own beliefs. One way to choose a course of action that is workable in the face of conflicting ethical demands is to use an ethical problem-solving process as a proactive tool for anticipating potential ethical problems in research or practice before they occur and then use the same guide as a systematic model for dealing with any unanticipated ethical problems or dilemmas as they occur in either research or practice. This book provides a clear understanding of the principles and processes for ethical conduct in anthropology, together with set of processes that can address problems as they occur.

## ANTHROPOLOGICAL CHALLENGES AND CULTURALLY SENSITIVE ETHICS

Anthropologists have an obligation both to challenge and to contribute to the advancement of research and practice ethics within the framework of evolving cultural theory and practice. Most anthropologists share concern over the dominance of Western philosophy in shaping international definitions, rules, and processes for ethical research. The grounding of research in the Western philosophies of positivism and modernism has resulted in rapid cultural changes over the past two centuries, especially in the area of technology and secularism taking precedence over sectarianism. At the same time, those Western philosophies have created many of the ethical dilemmas and challenges that anthropologists have faced for the past two centuries, while simultaneously giving rise to competing anthropological paradigms that challenge the more rules-based and more universalistic stance taken in the natural sciences.

We have constructed this book to encourage critical as well as constructive ethical thinking that allows researchers to simultaneously comply with, challenge, expand, and appropriately modify the core conditions that apply to ethical anthropological research, while accommodating alternative cultural viewpoints. The basic practices of ethical assessment are culturally and historically grounded, thereby not without biases, and need to be critically evaluated with cognizance of those biases and the way they are expressed.

Anthropologists are obligated to understand the philosophical basis for ethical problem-solving processes and realize the existence of theoretical and cultural challenges within the field of ethics, in particular, and crosscultural ethics, in general (Muller 1994). Muller points out that anthropological theory supports three primary contentions that must be addressed to resolve ethical dilemmas: (1) ethical dilemmas must be understood within their cultural context, not simply as a clash of "universal" principles, (2) all moral systems are culturally embedded and need to be understood as part of a complex whole, and (3) most bioethical problems have a multicultural character (1994:449).

The very nature of anthropological theory, however, suggests that once we move beyond our own cultural boundaries, the ethical principles and the conditions for their application may significantly change, producing even more ethical dilemmas for the researcher/practitioner.

Our approach to resolving some of these issues is to provide an overview of the cultural history of religious and ethical principles, to identify the consensual and significant modern ethical principles and processes that are commonly applied to anthropological research, and to offer a framework for exploring the intersection between the principles and the problems that need to be solved through the presentation of cases that explore ethical problems commonly encountered by anthropologists.

Chapter 2 introduces the history of ethics and the development of current research ethics. It draws on historical codes such as that of Hammurabi, the sixth king of Babylon who wrote one of the first known codes of ethics, and moves forward to the 2003 United Nations Guidelines for International Research. Chapter 3 introduces the reader to heart of the discussion—the basic principles in research and practice ethics—while chapters 4 and 5 provide descriptions of active processes for protecting subjects generated by the basic principles. Chapter 6 takes an in-depth look at the concept of vulnerable populations, and chapter 7 explains, in detail, the problem-solving guide we have created to allow readers to explore the critical viewpoints embedded in an ethical dilemma. It also introduces another problem-solving model in the ethical dilemma at the end of the chapter.

All chapters end with thought questions that stimulate individual exploration of the issues in the chapter, and selected chapters (2, 3, 4, 5, and 7) include a case that focuses on an issue explored in the chapter—a problematic situation that anthropologists could encounter, including the potential conflict between the values of being a researcher and also an advocate, the difficulty of combining or balancing the greatly valued concept of cultural relativism with the idea of universal ethics such as human rights, the dilemma of having to choose among ethical principles in conflict, and the dilemmas posed by a conflict between personal moral codes and ethical codes promulgated by professional disciplinary association. Each "ethical dilemma" case is accompanied by questions that stimulate critical thinking and problem solving, along with recommended resource material. The cases are designed to: (1) provide a ready-made way to approach ethics in the classroom, (2) introduce students to common dilemmas faced by anthropologists during research and practice, (3) demonstrate how the application of ethics can be used to unsnarl emotional and value-laden issues, and (4) facilitate the incorporation of ethical principles and guidelines into everyday life as well as professional decision making. All of the references cited within the text and listed at the end of the cases are excellent supplemental readings for the book as a whole.

## Thought Questions

1. Why are there multiple codes of ethics for anthropologists?

2. Compare the American Anthropological Association Principles of Professional Responsibility (see excerpts on pp. 6–7; the entire code can be found at http:www.aanet.org/stmts/ethstmnt.htm) with the National Association for the Practice of Anthropology Ethical Guidelines (http://www.practicinganthropology.org/about/?section=ethical_guidelines), and compare the Society for American Archaeology's Principles of Archaeological Ethics (http://www.saa.org/ABOUTSAA/COMMITTEES/ethics/principles.html) with the code for the World Archaeological Congress (http://www.worldarchaeologicalcongress.org/site/about_ethi.php).

   - What are the similarities between the codes?
   - What are some of the differences?
   - Which of the differences are produced by the differences between ethical issues surrounding research, versus ethical issues surrounding practice (such as teaching, consulting, working for a company, etc.)?
   - Which differences are produced by the subject matter of the research and the discipline within which the research is conducted (archaeology versus sociocultural research)?

3. Become conscious of how many times each day you make a decision that is rooted in your ethical framework. Make a list of each decision, what stimulated it, and what ideas you relied on in making it.

   - How many instances did you identify?
   - What kinds of situations forced you to make such decisions?
   - What was the source of the values you relied on in making those decisions—those of friend, parents, teachers, religion?
   - If you repeated the listing exercise on a different day, for instance, on the weekend, might you get different results? Why?

*Chapter Two*

---

# Legal Codes and
# Ethical Guidelines

---

> [The] basic anthropological tenet that all cultures have some
> degree of internal consistency and that many items of behavior
> and many customs form patterns and interrelationships . . . when
> translated into the realm of moral behavior [produces the assump-
> tion] that moral dilemmas and the means to resolve them cannot
> be separated from the institutional, political, economic, social, and
> cultural contexts in which they are embedded. (Muller 1994:452)

The concepts of moral behavior and living an ethical life are
deeply embedded in the overall cultural history of human beings. People tend to create rules for behavior and then find ways to reinforce or
enforce those rules in daily life. People also are very creative in avoiding, bending, breaking, or challenging those same rules. Throughout
human history, what was considered to be proper or moral behavior at a
given moment became intertwined with religion, politics, power, force,
and changing ideologies. The concept of ethics has often grown out of
and been reinforced by religious doctrine and secular political philosophies. Most of the principles for ethical behavior (e.g., respect others, do
no harm, be fair) are shared across very significant cultural boundaries; however, the interpretation of those principles and their application to groups within different cultures have been highly variable.

The focus of this book is to identify and explain basic ethical
principles in relation to anthropological research and practice. The
principles for ethical research have been established and agreed on for
some time both within single cultures and among many, but not all,
cultures. Generally the currently "agreed on" international research
ethics guidelines follow the ethics philosophy historically based in the

science found in Western cultures, even though ethics also has followed other cultural paths in non-Western cultures. While the authors recognize there are variations on the definition of *ethics,* the following provides the one employed in this book:

> Main Entry: eth·ic
> Pronunciation: 'e-thik
> Function: *noun*
> Etymology: Middle English *ethik,* from Middle French *ethique,* from Latin *ethice,* from Greek *ēthikē,* from *ēthikos*
> 1 *plural but singular or plural in construction*: the discipline dealing with what is good and bad and with moral duty and obligation
> 2 a: a set of moral principles: a theory or system of moral values <the present-day materialistic *ethic*> <an old-fashioned work *ethic*>—often used in plural but sing. or plural in constr. <an elaborate *ethics*> <Christian *ethics*> b *plural but singular or plural in construction*: the principles of conduct governing an individual or a group <professional *ethics*> c: a guiding philosophy d: a consciousness of moral importance [forge a conservation *ethic*]
> 3 *plural*: a set of moral issues or aspects (as rightness) <debated the *ethics* of human cloning> (*Merriam-Webster Online Dictionary:* http://www.m-w.com/dictionary/ethics).

The *Merriam-Webster* definition not only provides a clear explanation for what the concept means, but it also provides some insight into two other key elements in our exploration of anthropological ethics: (1) the existence of multiple ethical systems, both within cultures and among cultures; and (2) the fact that ethics are embedded in key cultural institutions such as religion, politics, economics, work, and legal systems (Christian ethics, conservative ethics, materialist ethics, professional ethics, and dealing with what is good and bad). The definition is also useful for exploring the history of ethics as well as understanding what constitutes "modern" ethics. A gradual evolution and expansion of ethical research principles has occurred in response to new social, religious, and political ideologies, in addition to the unanticipated changes in technology, science, and law. "Ethics is the concept of balancing benefits and risks of choices and decisions. The underlying heritage of ethics can be seen in all cultures, religions, and in ancient writings from around the world" (Macer 1994).

At the same time, differences of opinion persist when local cultural, philosophical, legal, and religious precedents conflict with competing cultural, legal, philosophical, religious, and ethical rationales within national and across international boundaries.

## ETHICS DIDN'T START WITH SCIENCE

The whole subject of ethics has been a key area of philosophical exploration and discussion with both secular and sacred traditions, before and after the development of science. Science and its accompanying paradigm for scientific research is a historically recent cultural activity that significantly expanded with the development of positivist philosophy and the creation of the scientific method. A large portion of the scientific revolution of the past couple of centuries has been devoted to exploring the physical and biological world first, and exploring the social and cultural domains of human existence second. Before the philosophy of science and the idea of research existed, there were a large number of culturally grounded ethical principles, guidelines, mores, rules, and laws that governed how human beings were supposed to treat one another. Most of those ethical "understandings" were carried over into research ethics in accord with the basic cultural orientations of the researchers. However, religiously based ethics and rules of behavior have also been present and have guided behavior in culturally specific ways throughout recorded history; the influence of that part of human history is crucial to a thorough understanding of research ethics.

### Hammurabi Tried Casting It in Stone

The sixth king of Babylon, Hammurabi, is often credited with producing the first written legal principles. Hammurabi's Code was literally written in stone in cuneiform script in a language called Akkadian. This act is one of several important historical precedents for creating systematic and consensual (rather than idiosyncratic or individually authoritative) legal codes throughout the world. It allows a culture to develop a rules-based system of social control, distinguishes culturally acceptable good behavior from bad behavior, and provides guidelines for enforcement of good behavior.

The basic premise of uniform legal codes is that complex societies need agreed-upon guidelines for dealing with human behavior that violates established law and the boundaries of established authority. Hammurabi's efforts (c. 1780 B.C.) were based on codifying earlier Sumerian law, and his laws and decrees are a primary historic example of the process that has turned into the current emphasis in many cultures on the rule of law. The actual laws Hammurabi publicly distributed were embedded in both the religious and the civil culture of Babylon at that time, and they focus on four primary areas that include family law (marriage and family relationships), economic law (recompense for work, cost of services) civil law (legal functions, disputes), and criminal law (murder, theft, injury).

The primary basis for judgment and justice that is codified in the laws is the concept of reciprocal treatment and enforcement (sometimes called "tit for tat" or "an eye for an eye"). A total of 282 legal precepts are recorded in the L. W. King translation of the Akkadian tablets (King 2004). The following provides examples of Hammurabi's laws that we have deliberately chosen to provide a contrast to U.S. legal systems (from King 2004:1910):

### Excerpts: Hammurabi's Code of Laws and Royal Decrees

#### Family Law (Divorce)

137. If a man wishes to separate from a woman who has borne him children, or from his wife who has borne him children: then he shall give that wife her dowry, and a part of the usufruct of field, garden, and property, so that she can rear her children. When she has brought up her children, a portion of all that is given to the children, equal as that of one son, shall be given to her. She may then marry the man of her heart.

138. If a man wishes to separate from his wife who has borne him no children, he shall give her the amount of her purchase money and the dowry that she brought from her father's house, and let her go.

141. If a man's wife, who lives in his house, wishes to leave it, plunges into debt, tries to ruin her house, neglects her husband, and is judicially convicted: if her husband offers her release, she may go on her way, and he gives her nothing as a gift of release. If her husband does not wish to release her, and if he takes another wife, she shall remain as servant in her husband's house.

195. If a son strikes his father, his hands shall be hewn off.

#### Economic Law (Debt)

117. If any one fail to meet a claim for debt, and sell himself, his wife, his son, and daughter for money or give them away to forced labor: they shall work for three years in the house of the man who bought them, or the proprietor, and in the fourth year they shall be set free.

#### Civil Law (Challenge to Authority, Reciprocal Justice)

5. If a judge try a case, reach a decision, and present his judgment in writing; if later error shall appear in his decision, and it be through his own fault, then he shall pay twelve times the fine set by him in the case, and he shall be publicly removed from the judge's bench, and never again shall he sit there to render judgment.

196. If a man put out the eye of another man, his eye shall be put out. [An eye for an eye]

197. If he breaks another man's bone, his bone shall be broken.

198. If he put out the eye of a freed man, or break the bone of a freed man, he shall pay one gold mina.

199. If he put out the eye of a man's slave, or break the bone of a man's slave, he shall pay one-half of its value.

200. If a man knock out the teeth of his equal, his teeth shall be knocked out. [A tooth for a tooth]

201. If he knocks out the teeth of a freed man, he shall pay one-third of a gold mina.

202. If any one strikes the body of a man higher in rank than he, he shall receive sixty blows with an ox-whip in public.

**Criminal Law (Social Structure and Punishment, Slavery)**

8. If any one steal cattle or sheep, or an ass, or a pig or a goat, if it belongs to a god or to the court, the thief shall pay thirtyfold; if they belonged to a freed man of the king he shall pay tenfold; if the thief has nothing with which to pay he shall be put to death.

15. If any one takes a male or female slave of the court, or a male or female slave of a freed man, outside the city gates, he shall be put to death.

16. If any one receive into his house a runaway male or female slave of the court, or of a freedman, and does not bring it out at the public proclamation of the major domus, the master of the house shall be put to death.

In Hammurabi's time, slavery was not only allowed, it was sanctioned by both religious authority and the civil authority; the religious and cultural codes of ethics allowed for differential treatment of men and women in terms of legal and property rights; the system allowed authority to be challenged, but with very severe consequences to either the challenger or the challenged, depending on the outcome; and the existing social stratification was strongly supported by different treatment for people of different social statuses—justice was not blind, it was class-based.

While many of the specific rulings and laws have changed as cultures, religions, and ethical principles have changed through time, our current ethical guidelines for research and practice can be traced to this historic need to put principles in writing, so they are standardized rather than being the whim of the individual in power. Ethical rules reflect and reify the cultures that produce them. The historical and cultural foundation for ethical principles and guidelines in the United States has evolved from early Greek philosophical writings, through the Bill of Rights in the United States Constitution, to present-day law. The early history of civil law is commonly attributed to Roman law and continues as a civil tradition through time. These philosophical and legal foundations are important to understanding the basic ethical principles for human research, even though they were not enough to prevent human abuses that were incorrectly produced in the name of science.

## Religion and Ethics

At the same time, it is important to understand the contribution of religion to ethics and ethical principles and to understand some potential points of cultural conflict between secular (civil) law and ethics and religious law and ethical guidelines. There has been a frequent conflation between religious and secularly based ethics throughout human history. Religiously based moral guidelines and philosophical principles have produced many of the commonly agreed on basic concepts, values, and beliefs that are the foundation for current research ethics guidelines. Religious differences, however, have also produced some of the current ethical debates about research, research ethics, and the basic parameters of human rights and civil rights within and across cultural boundaries.

Two of the most commonly discussed religiously based legal and ethical systems in effect in different parts of the world are Halakha (Jewish law) and Shari'ah (Islamic law). The two are briefly presented here as a point of comparison with the secularized research and practice of ethical guidelines presented in later chapters. Both of these ethical systems have had a direct impact on anthropologists who have conducted ethnographic research among cultural groups who practice these moral principles. In return, both have had an impact on the discussions and debates about proper ethical guidelines for anthropological research and practice ethics policy and guidelines.

### Excerpts: Summaries of Halakha (Jewish) and Shari'ah (Islamic) Religious Law

#### Halakha

Halakha is the collective corpus of Jewish religious law, including biblical law (the 613 mitzvot) and later talmudic and rabbinic law as well as customs and traditions. Judaism classically draws no distinction in its laws between religious and nonreligious life. Hence, Halakha guides not only religious practices and beliefs, but numerous aspects of day-to-day life. Halakha is often translated as "Jewish Law," though a more accurate translation might be "the path" or "the way of walking." The word is derived from the Hebrew root that means "to go, to walk or to travel."

The Ten Commandments, or Decalogue, are a list of religious and moral imperatives which, according to the Hebrew Bible, were written by God and given to Moses on Mount Sinai in the form of two stone tablets. They feature prominently in Judaism, Christianity and Islam. The phrase "Ten Commandments" generally refers to the broadly identical passages in Exodus 20:2–17 and Deuteronomy 5:6–21:

I. I am the Lord thy God; thou shalt have no other gods before me.
II. Thou shalt not take the name of the Lord thy God in vain.
III. Remember the Sabbath day, to keep it holy.
IV. Honor thy father and thy mother.
V. Thou shalt not kill.
VI. Thou shalt not commit adultery.
VII. Thou shalt not steal.
VIII. Thou shalt not bear false witness against thy neighbor.

IX. Thou shalt not covet thy neighbor's house.

X. Thou shalt not covet thy neighbor's wife, nor his manservant, nor his maidservant, nor his ox, nor his ass, nor anything that is thy neighbor's.

## Shari'ah

Total and unqualified submission to the will of Allah (God) is the fundamental tenet of Islam: Islamic law is therefore the expression of Allah's command for Muslim society and, in application, constitutes a system of duties that are incumbent upon a Muslim by virtue of his religious belief. Known as the Shari'ah (literally, "the path leading to the watering place"), the law constitutes a divinely ordained path of conduct that guides the Muslim toward a practical expression of his religious conviction in this world and the goal of divine favour in the world to come.

### Nature and significance of Islamic law

Muslim jurisprudence, the science of ascertaining the precise terms of the Shari'ah, is known as *fiqh* (literally "understanding"). The historical process of the discovery of Allah's law (see below) was regarded as completed by the end of the ninth century when the law had achieved a definitive formulation in a number of legal manuals written by different jurists. Throughout the medieval period this basic doctrine was elaborated and systematized in a large number of commentaries, and the voluminous literature thus produced constitutes the traditional textual authority of Shari'ah law.

In classical form the Shari'ah differs from Western systems of law in two principal respects. In the first place the scope of the Shari'ah is much wider, since it regulates man's relationship not only with his neighbours and with the state, which is the limit of most other legal systems, but also with his God and his own conscience. Ritual practices, such as the daily prayers, almsgiving, fasting, and pilgrimage, are an integral part of Shari'ah law and usually occupy the first chapters in the legal manuals. The Shari'ah is also concerned as much with ethical standards as with legal rules, indicating not only what man is entitled or bound to do in law, but also what he ought, in conscience, to do or refrain from doing. Accordingly, certain acts are classified as praiseworthy (*mandub*), which means that their performance brings divine favour and their omission divine disfavour, and others as blameworthy (*makruh*), which means that omission brings divine favour and commission divine disfavour; but in neither case is there any legal sanction of punishment or reward, nullity or validity. The Shari'ah is not merely a system of law, but a comprehensive code of behaviour that embraces both private and public activities.

The second major distinction between the Shari'ah and Western legal systems is the result of the Islamic concept of law as the expression of the divine will. With the death of the Prophet Muhammad in 632, communication of the divine will to man ceased so that the terms of the divine revelation were henceforth fixed and immutable. When, therefore, the process of interpretation and expansion of this source material was held to be complete with the crystallization of the doctrine in the medieval legal manuals, Shari'ah law became a rigid and static system. Unlike secular legal systems that grow out of society and change with the changing circumstances of society, Shari'ah law was imposed upon society from above. In Islamic jurisprudence it is not society that moulds and fashions the law, but the law that precedes and controls society.

*The substance of traditional Shari'ah law*
Shari'ah duties are broadly divided into those that an individual owes to Allah (the ritual practices or *'ibadat*) and those that he owes to his fellow men (*mu'amalat*).

The ritual duties that are sanctioned by Shari'ah law generally fall into five categories: (1) laws on ritual purity, (2) laws about the appropriate forms and content of prayers and praying, (3) ritual observances and calendars (such as fasting), (4) appropriate forms of charity toward others, and (5) making a holy pilgrimage to Mecca. The laws governing the treatment of others are focused on eight aspects of human interaction. These are (1) laws about economic and financial exchange, (2) inheritance rules and laws, (3) familial law (marriage, divorce, child care), (4) culinary or dietary laws (how to prepare food, acceptable foods and beverages, etc.), (5) a code of punishments and principles for punishment, (6) laws for times of warfare, (7) laws for times of peace, (8) and a code of judicial conduct (acceptable kinds of evidence, behavior of witnesses, etc.). (*Encyclopedia Britannica* 2008, pp. 1 and 5. http://www.britannica.com/eb/article-9105857/Shariah [Accessed Jan. 21, 2008.])

There are some clear historical and philosophical similarities between these two legal systems. Both merge (or do not distinguish between) civil and religious conditions, and there is a limited separation of church and state compared to many other legal systems. The two systems have principles and punishments for violation of both the ethics of everyday life and the ethics of religious observance. The basic principles in Halakha and Shari'ah legal systems point out some significant differences between current civil and secular legal systems, compared with religious legal systems. In the former, there has been a gradual reduction in culturally approved discrimination on the basis of gender, cultural or racial origin, religious affiliation, or economic status. In the sacred systems, certain forms of institutionalized discrimination are deeply embedded, allowed, and even prioritized. Both of these religiously based legal systems involve differential rights and differential treatment given to recognized members of the religion, as opposed to all others. Some individuals (e.g., women) are not recognized as having the same rights to equal treatment within the religious groups, and anyone "not of the religion" may also be considered an appropriate target of discriminatory practices (e.g., the concept of

Dhimmitude in Shari'ah law). Dhimmitude is the legal treatment of non-Muslims under Shari'ah law and involves a tax specifically targeted at non-Muslims and various forms of identification and treatment in terms of legal rights (cf. Yeor et al. 2001). These proscriptions and practices are one of the elements in these types of moral systems that create crosscultural ethical dilemmas for researchers who are working in such cultures.

The concept of Dhimmitude in Shari'ah law can be seen as a crosscultural challenge to the international secular trend in ethics to accept diversity and difference both within and between cultures. It is an example of the culturally and religiously sanctioned discrimination against nonbelievers and against other religions that is a very common feature found in most of the world's major religions.

In Israel, the ongoing discussion over the legal and ethical standing of rabbinical courts in relation to the national court system is an example of a "within the culture" ethical debate (Rayner 1998). The following excerpt (Shahak 1995:18, 119) points up some of the concerns over the use of religiously based rulings that impact the national legal system, which is much more secular in design and principle.

> The rabbis of Safad, joined by the Chief Rabbi Bakshi-Doron, recently issued a judgment prohibiting Jews living in the Land of Israel to lease or sell any real estate property to non-Jews. These rabbis are on the State of Israel's payroll. Yet all too clearly, their judgment contravenes Israeli state laws proscribing public expressions of racism and utterances hurtful to human dignity.
>
> Nonetheless, the rabbis of Safad did not invent this prohibition. The racist ruling is part and parcel of Jewish religious law (*halacha*). Furthermore, all the rulings of Jewish religious law concerning non-Jews, and incidentally, also Jewish women and some other Jewish sectors, are racist and discriminatory. Yet for years such rulings have been routinely invoked by rabbinical courts which are a recognized part of the State of Israel's judiciary.
>
> Two examples show what the application of such laws may involve. According to Jewish religious law, both non-Jews and Jewish women cannot validly testify in rabbinical courts. True, Jewish women are permitted to testify in a few strictly limited matters considered "female affairs." If a case involves "a major judicial effort," however, a Jewish woman's testimony is perforce invalid, because "all women are lazy by nature." But even in cases not involving a "major judicial effort" when Jewish women can testify, a problem appears when the testimony of a Jewish woman is contradicted by the testimony of a Jewish man. Jewish religious law solves this problem by the formula that "a testimony of 100 Jewish women is equivalent to a testimony of a single Jewish man."

Both of these legal and ethical systems are culturally congruent with the beliefs of the cultures that endorse religion as part of their legal systems, but both are in conflict with the international consensus about the equal treatment humans regardless of gender, origin, or religious affiliation. Each of these systems (and other sectarian legal systems) produces potential ethical dilemmas for crosscultural researchers who want to conduct both culturally and ethically appropriate research. As a consequence, the gradual evolution of secular and civil law, with important cultural clashes between secular and sacred law throughout history, has framed the more recent history of the evolution of research ethics guidelines. In most cases, the ethical principles are compatible with many of the basic religious principles, and there is a clear consensus that cultural variation in religious belief and expression deserves both respect and accommodation but that the more discriminatory practices embedded in religious, legal, and ethical systems are not appropriate in a multinational, multicultural context.

## LEST HISTORY REPEAT ITSELF

Ethical disasters appear to be the primary impetus for creating ethical guidelines for human research. The creation of both national and international ethical guidelines has generally occurred when there have been very serious ethical breaches due to the way that a small group or an individual scientist has misapplied science or to a rogue nation that has supported unethical human experimentation or torture. Often following the instance of some horrendous activity, the ethical guidelines are revised, made clearer, and often made more stringent.

Without doubt there were many documented ethical lapses in human research prior to World War II (Lederer 1995). These lapses, or breaches, were the impetus for much of the current ethics guidelines shaping human subjects research and practice that emerged after the Nuremberg trials of Nazi war criminals. As Barbara Rylko-Bauer and others have pointed out, there is a political economy of brutality, often done in the name of science, conducted against marginalized and disenfranchised populations that are unable to protect themselves (Paul Farmer et al., n.d.). While this type of brutality is as old as political dominance, during and following the Nazi genocide against Gypsies, Jews, Poles, and many others, it became more fully documented than ever before.

Following the Nuremberg trials, what became known as the Nuremberg Code (1947) was developed and has become the basis for many international codes of treatment of human populations since then. In terms of human subjects research, and to a lesser extent, practice, those primary international codes include: Draft Code of Ethics on

Experimentation (1961), Helsinki Declaration (1964), United Nations CIOMS Research Ethics Guidelines (1981), International Guidelines: Ethics and Research on Human Subjects (1993), and United Nations Revision of International Guidelines CIOMS (2002). Each of these declarations, codes, treaties, and guidelines added something new to the ethics of research, and on rare occasions, removed an element.

## Nuremberg (1947)

The precursor to the creation of the Nuremberg Code were the Nuremberg War Crimes trials that focused on the actions of soldiers and civilians in the Nazi death camps during World War II, where prisoners were experimented on and tortured for the primary purpose of physical, biological, and medical research designed to enhance the position of the Axis Power (Annas and Grodin 1991). The Nuremberg trials that followed the defeat of the Axis Powers were one of the first incidences in which unethical human research was officially and internationally recognized as a crime against humanity. World War II produced a tremendous surge in physical, biological, and medical research that was primarily directed at finding ways to win the war. Part of that effort was directed at medical research on biological weapons. But a considerable part of it was also directed at experimentation that was indistinguishable from torture and conducted on political prisoners in the Nazi labor camps. These experiments were thoroughly documented in the Nuremberg War Crimes trials.

The most famous were the Mengela Experiments. The findings from the war crimes tribunal, coupled with international public outrage and fear of this kind of violation of religious and secular ethical codes, produced the first formal international guidelines for ethical biomedical research on human subjects. The Nuremberg Code subsequently governed basic ethics on experimentation, especially medical experimentation.

### Basic Elements of the Nuremberg Code 1947

1. Voluntary consent is required for all research participants.
2. The participant must have the legal capacity to give consent.
3. The consent must be free from coercion or deceit.
4. Researchers have the primary responsibility for maintaining the ethics of the research.
5. An individual's participation can be terminated at anytime during the research.
6. The research should yield results that are for the common good.
7. No unnecessary research should be conducted.
9. Research should be based on results of previous research or knowledge.
10. No unnecessary physical or mental suffering or injury should result from the research.

11. The research should be conducted by scientifically qualified persons.

12. If the benefit does not outweigh the risks or harms of the research, the research should not be conducted.

The focal point for the Nuremberg Code was the requirement for voluntary participation, for informed consent, and for the benefits of the research to outweigh the risks or harms of the research—three issues that have remained central to all research ethics codes from that time on, with some inevitable changes in definitions and cultural understandings (Katz 1991).

## Helsinki (1961, 1964)

The late 1950s and early 1960s was a time of considerable turmoil and conflicting ethical debate over human rights, racism, and nuclear war. The United Nations was being debated and established. A nuclear arms race was producing the global tensions referred to as the cold war. Regional conflicts were turning into proxy global conflicts, like the Vietnam War.

One of the tools used to address some of these issues (especially the threat of nuclear disaster) at an international level was to strengthen and expand the international ethical guidelines for human research. There were three major national and international incidents that acted as a precipitating force to improve the international guidelines for protecting human subjects from harmful experimentation. In February, 1954, the Castle Bravo nuclear test (open air explosion) resulted in large amounts of nuclear fallout in the Marshall Islands near a nuclear test site in the Pacific. Medical monitoring of the local populations indicated that many of the exposed Marshall Islanders contracted a much higher rate of cancers and a higher incidence of birth defects than otherwise would be expected (Johnston 2007).

In addition, the crew of a Japanese fishing boat was exposed to the radiation fallout and at least one of the crew members died from radiation sickness (Hacker 1994). This above-ground nuclear test produced extensive international attention and fear. Another precipitating condition—a critical lapse in ethical standards—that helped to fuel the Helsinki Accord was the experiment in which U.S., British, and Canadian soldiers were ordered to witness (and be exposed to) above-ground nuclear explosions, to determine the radiation effects of exposure to nuclear bombs on the human beings at the Nevada nuclear test sites, among other places. Another precipitating condition was a report on the direct injection of radioactive substances into uninformed and nonvoluntary human patients in some medical facilities, documented by the ACHRE (U.S. Department of Energy Advisory Committee on Human Radiation Experiments 1996) report excerpted below.

### ACHRE Report on Human Radiation Experiments

From 1945 through 1947 Manhattan Project researchers injected eighteen human subjects with plutonium, five human subjects with polonium, and six human subjects with uranium to obtain metabolic data related to the safety of those working on the production of nuclear weapons. All of these subjects were patients hospitalized at facilities affiliated with the Universities of Rochester, California, and Chicago or at Oak Ridge. Another set of experiments took place between 1953 and 1957 at Massachusetts General Hospital, in which human subjects were injected with uranium. In no case was there any expectation that these patient-subjects would benefit medically from the injections . . .

With one exception, the historical record suggests that these patients-subjects were not told that they were to be used in experiments for which there was no expectation they would benefit medically, and as a consequence, it is unlikely they consented to this use of their person. (http://hss.energy.gov/healthsafety/ohre/roadmap/achre/index.html)

Out of this shameful, but not unusual, use of a captured audience came another push toward what became the creation of the Helsinki Accord. In the following pages we review how the Helsinki Accord extended the framework for experimentation on human subjects from previous guidelines.

### Helsinki Accord 1964:
### Improvements in Ethical Guidelines for Research

**Key points in the guidelines:**

1. There must be an independent ethical committee to oversee the research on human beings (i.e., a review board).
2. The rights of individuals outweigh the benefits to society.
3. An informants' privacy must be protected.
4. The results of research need to be accurately preserved.
5. Every patient, including controls must receive the best standard of care during the research.
6. There is a difference between research and practice (professional care).

**New elements added:**

1. The Accord establishes the importance of the individual and expands the ethical code to other research endeavors, not just medical research.
2. The Accord establishes need for an independent committee to oversee the experimental protocol in order to conform with the laws and regulations of the country where research is to be conducted.
3. The guidelines establish a precedent that individual human concerns outweigh the importance of the research to society and science.
4. Participants' privacy must be accommodated.
5. The researcher is obligated to preserve accurate data for review.

6. The Accord establishes the principle of informed consent: participants must be informed of the aims, methods, benefits and risks of participating before agreeing to participate.

7. Every participant including control group patients has the right to be provided with the best proven diagnostic and therapeutic standard of treatment.

The Helsinki Accord provided improved definitions for many aspects of human subjects protection in research, and it documented the beginning of the international political movement for universal human rights as well as the movement to establish the rights of the individual over society or government. It also signals the beginnings of an overall concern for distributive justice (the fair allocation of resources among diverse members of society) in research ethics. We continue our overview of the guidelines developed since then and identify how each reframed rights in terms of the larger and changing world context.

## International Ethical Guidelines for Biomedical Research Involving Human Subjects (1993)

The next extensive debate and discussion over international guidelines was a response to ethical issues tied to the widening gap in power and resources between developed and developing nations, symbolized by the ethical problems raised by large-scale trials of vaccines and drugs, transnational research, and experimentation involving vulnerable population groups (Christkis and Panner 1991; CIOMS 1993). There were growing discrepancies in how previous ethical principles/ guidelines should be applied to research in other developing countries where socioeconomic circumstances and laws were radically different from those of industrialized nations. The power and resource differentials raised the specter of ethical exploitations. As a result, international ethics guidelines were developed as a response to crosscultural differences among researchers, sponsors, community members, and participants to protect these groups' interests.

### CIOMS 1993 Guidelines for
### Biomedical Research Involving Human Subjects
**Key points in the guidelines:**

1. Ethical research must take into account participants' culture(s), socioeconomic circumstances, national laws, and executive and administrative arrangement of his/her country.

2. The rights of vulnerable groups were highlighted, especially pregnant women, AIDS/HIV infected people, prisoners and the elderly.

3. The guidelines primarily protect the rights and welfare of human subjects of biomedical research.

4. The guidelines establish the international application of three main principles from The Belmont Report: respect for persons, beneficence and justice.

5. A number of procedures for safe-guarding confidentiality and ways of treating and compensating injured subjects are clarified.

**New elements added:**

1. The guidelines identify vulnerable groups that need special protection: children, people with mental disorders, women, and prisoners.

2. The guidelines establish the need to identify the responsibility of sponsors and host countries.

3. The guidelines recommend compensation for inconvenience, expenses, and time spent participating in the research, as standard practice.

4. The guidelines create protocols to protect subjects in underdeveloped communities.

6. A participant's right to treatment or compensation if injured during or from research is established.

7. The responsibilities of ethical review committees are clarified.

8. The guidelines establish the precedent for acquiring ascent from children and consent from child's guardians to participate in research.

It is worth noting that these guidelines do not define or discuss the difference between research and practice. With that omission, the guidelines become more clearly focused on research ethics, as opposed to the general ethics of praxis by researchers or others. The abandonment of the commentary on practice produced some confusion over what constituted acceptable or best practices, and it also allowed professional organizations to define ethical practice separately from ethical research, since the two were not in complete synchronization in most fields. The guidelines also de-emphasized social and behavioral research and, as a consequence, provided only limited guidance for dealing with the research ethics of nonmedical prevention and intervention research. While the CIOMS guidelines were a welcome addition, many of the power differential practices involved in pharmaceutical trials continued (Petryna 2005).

## International Ethical Guidelines for Biomedical Research Involving Human Subjects (2002)

The international guidelines were revised again in 2002 when the biomedical community (and bioethics paradigms) took the dominant role in the exploration and discussion of ethical practices in human research. Social, cultural, and behavioral research on humans was mentioned and discussed, but the contention that social science research was substantially different (or should have substantially different ethical principles and practices) was basically rejected by the international biomedical establishment. In a number of ways, the revisions appear to be more of a continuing international dialogue on the previous set of guidelines—and some subsequent refinement of the consensus—rather than a strong departure from the earlier guidelines. The 2002 guidelines, however, are a response to significant technological advances in human research, including issues surrounding the human genome project and an explosion of both genetic and clinical research trials taking place in Third World countries.

### CIOMS 2002 Guidelines for
### Biomedical Research Involving Human Subjects

**Key elements of guidelines:**

1. Refines the earlier discussion of vulnerable groups such as pregnant women, children, individuals with mental or behavioral disorders, and prisoners.

2. Expands the discussion of obligations to subjects, sponsors, and investigators, rather than just governments and sponsors.

3. Expands the discussion of the ethics of research in populations with limited resources and the risks that they maybe exposed to because of their situation.

**New elements added:**

1. The obligations and restrictions when conducting research with populations with limited resources are extended.

2. The ethics of when placebos may be used in research are discussed.

3. The need for a focus on women as research participants, especially women of a reproductive age is emphasized.

4. The obligations to external sponsors to provide health care services to participants are clarified or reinforced.

5. It identifies sponsors' and investigators' obligations to make every effort to ensure that populations and communities with limited resources will have the product, intervention or knowledge made available to them for their benefit.

When researchers become too narrowly focused on their own activities, they may fail to take into account the international context for their research (CIOMS 2002). The research ethics guidelines described above are just part of the ethical responsibilities for both research and praxis in international settings. The United Nations has invested its member nations' time in creating ethical guidelines for many activities that cross international and cultural boundaries. Research ethics must be viewed and understood in the context of the principles and guidelines discussed below, which are part of the treaty promises made by the United States government in relation to the ethical treatment of all human beings.

## ETHICAL GUIDELINES FOR
## RESEARCH IN THE UNITED STATES

The United States actively participated, and even (at times) took a leadership role, in the development of the international research ethics guidelines that are described in the previous section, and the overall U.S. stance on ethical guidelines for research should be viewed in that context. The revelations of several nationally horrifying ethical failures, however, also caused the U.S. federal government to create a set of national standards that apply to research ethics in addition to (and often beyond) the international standards. The first major set of principles and guidelines were produced by the national uproar in 1972 that followed the public acknowledgement of what became known as the Tuskegee experiments.

## Tuskegee

The Tuskegee experiment was conducted at Tuskegee University in Alabama (King 1992). The university is a historically black college and one of the first medical schools in the country to admit African American students. The Tuskegee experiment was implemented in 1932 at the urging of governmentally sponsored scientists (from the institution that later became the Center for Disease Control and Prevention [CDC]) in collaboration with the faculty at Tuskegee medical school. The purpose of the study was to document the natural course of syphilis in men. The researchers collected data on 399 African American men in Alabama over the course of many years. None of these men were told they were infected with syphilis, and none of them were treated for the disease (in order to study the natural course of the disease), even though effective treatments were available and even though those men would infect any sexual partners they might have in the course of their lives. This ethical failure had a powerful effect by decreasing the level of trust most minority communities have toward the federal government and federally funded medical science.

One result of the public outrage in response to the Tuskegee experiment was the establishment of a federally mandated and funded National Commission for the Protection of Human Subjects involved in research in the United States (http://ohsr.od.nih.gov/guidelines/index.html). That commission, made up of prominent citizens, clergy, scientists, ethicists, and members of minority and other vulnerable communities, not only identified a set of guidelines for research on vulnerable populations, but it also identified the fundamental principles that should guide all federally funded research on humans. Those definitions and principles became the basis for all subsequent laws, rules, regulations, and guidelines for human research in the United States and had a powerful impact on the international guidelines for human research as well.

The most important formal publication the commission produced was The Belmont Report, which established the principles that must guide all federally funded human research in the United States (http://ohsr.od.nih.gov/guidelines/belmont.html).

### The Belmont Report: Highlights

- The report expands the definition of research and includes the ideas that behavioral research needs to be subjected to ethical review, rather than just biomedical research.
- The report establishes a distinction between definitions of clinical practice and research.
- The report identifies and defines three critical ethical principles (respect for persons, beneficence, and justice) and consequently creates operating principles for judging ethical and unethical research.
- The report discusses the problem of the potential need for some form of mild deception in research where full disclosure would impair the validity of an experiment if a participant were to disclose all information up front in the consent process. It proposes allowing for deception if truly necessary for validity of research, assuming that the research meets the principles set out in the report. (http://www.hhs.gov/ohrp/humansubjects/guidance/belmont.htm)

## The U.S. Legal Basis for Human Subjects Protection

Two significant legislative actions—the Civil Rights Act of 1964 and the Privacy and Confidentiality Act of 1974—established the rights of individual citizens in the United States, including their right to protection, even as research subjects. The ethical guidelines for human research in the U.S. take into account the following laws and policies, in addition to the regulations for review.

### Key Laws and Policies Protecting Human Subjects in Research

- Civil Rights Act of 1964. Document Number: PL 88-352 Date: 02 JUL 64 88th Congress, H. R. 7152.
- The Privacy Act of 1974. 5 U.S.C. § 552a As Amended.
- Bureau of Medical Services Circular no. 38, 23 June 1966 U.S. Public Health Service required formal review of the ethics of research supported by the Public Health Service. Surgeon General, Public Health Service to the Heads of the Institutions Conducting Research with Public Health Service Grants, 8 February 1966 ("Clinical research and investigation involving human beings") (ACHRE No. HHS-090794-A). This policy was distributed through Bureau of Medical Services Circular no. 38, 23 June 1966 ("Clinical Investigations Using Human Beings As Subjects") (ACHRE No. HHS-090794-A).
- 1971 DHEW The Institutional Guide to DHEW Policy on Protection of Human Subjects. U.S. Department of Health, Education, and Welfare (Washington, D.C.: GPO, 1971) (ACHRE No. HHS-090794-A).
- 1974 Formal establishment of IRBs (Institutional Review Boards) Protection of Human Subjects, 39 Fed. Reg. 105, 18914–18920 (1974) (to be codified at 45 CFR-46.

- 1974 National Research Act: Established the National Commission for the Protection of Human Subjects. National Research Act of 1974. P.L. 348, 93d Cong., 2d Sess. (12 July 1974).
- 1981 Final regulations issued by Department of Health and Human Services.
- 1990 Titles I and V of the Americans with Disabilities Act of 1990 (Pub. L. 101–336) (ADA).
- Health Insurance Portability and Accountability Act of 1996 ("HIPAA") Pub. L. 104–191.
- 2005 Most Recent Revisions for Protection of Human Subjects (45 CFR-46).

These laws and regulations require that an ethical review be conducted to determine whether anyone is put at risk by any federally funded research that includes living humans. These laws also establish guaranteed protections for privacy, confidentiality of records and data, protection from undue harm, and social justice for research projects. The full scope of the U.S. regulations for human subjects protection can be found at hhs.gov/ohrp/humansubjects/guidance/45cfr46.htm.

## Institutional Review Boards (IRBs)

One of the most powerful (and perhaps most problematic for social science research) legislative and administrative results from the Tuskegee experiment was the establishment of formal ethical research review boards that review all research directed at human beings through a decentralized ethical review process intended to include local community participation and values. The U.S. Congress and the Public Health Service began to establish formal ethical reviews earlier than the revelation of the Tuskegee experiment in order to be compliant with the international guidelines, but they radically improved and expanded the review procedures after the exposure of the Tuskegee violations. The regulations governing the review of human subjects protections in research projects is called 45 CFR-46, or Title 45 of the Code of Federal Regulations (CFR) for Public Welfare (DHHS, National Institutes of Health, Office for Protection of Human Subjects), Part 46 Protection of Human Subjects. It is also sometimes called the common rules because these same rules are registered for virtually all of the other federal agencies that support any form of research. These federal regulations require that any institution in the United States that receives federal funding and conducts research must have a duly constituted Institutional Review Board, or must have access to an IRB in another institution that can review the ethics of the proposed research. Research projects must include documentation by the IRB that the following conditions are addressed and adhered to regardless of the nature of the research (45 CFR-46), hence the difficulties often encountered by nonmedically invasive social science researchers.

### IRB: Conditions to Evaluate for Proposed Research

**Sound Research Design.** Faulty research design is unethical because it cannot produce defensible or legitimate results; there is wide latitude in research methods as long as they follow established, documented, scientific protocols.

**Protection of Confidentiality.** People have the right to protect their privacy and have it protected by researchers; this includes provision for data storage, data protection; and protection of participant identity.

**Equality in Treatment of Subjects.** The risks and rewards for the research must be balanced and equitable; the selection process for participation should be fair and equitable.

**Consideration of Risks/benefits.** There must be a serious exploration and mitigation of the risks and benefits associated with the research; most common risks to be considered include physical harm, social harm, and psychological harm.

**Monitoring of Data Collection.** There must be a process for determining if the research was conducted ethically; the research cannot be done in secret without oversight; often there are provisions for disposition of the data in the future.

**Documentation of Informed Consent.** The participant must be informed of any risks they might encounter and an appropriate process for informed consent must be established, documented, and conducted; written informed consent is most common condition, but the law allows alternate forms of documentation if written informed consent would put subjects as risk.

**Participation is Voluntary.** There must be good documentation that no social, economic, or psychological coercion occurred and that participation is voluntary.

The basic requirement that has evolved over time is that all institutionally based sociocultural research should also be submitted to and approved by an IRB, including unfunded research (Bradburd 2006). This requirement has created a mixture of compliance, controversy, and resistance on the part of social science groups, including anthropologists (Boster 2006). As Ribeiro points out, "Two key issues have been especially problematic for anthropologists: first, professional competency of IRBs to evaluate anthropological protocols; and second, applications of requirements for informed consent" (2006:529). The former issue has to be addressed by educating local and national IRBs about anthropological research methods and protocols, as in the following:

> Cultural anthropologists often face difficulties when research protocols are submitted to IRBs for approval, particularly when they must be reviewed by IRBs within biomedical settings. IRBs may be unfamiliar with anthropological methods such as ethnography and other qualitative methodologies. Additionally, anthropologists may work with populations in national or international settings where written informed consent is problematic because of the

nature of the study, illiteracy, or the social vulnerability of the participants. (Fluehr-Lobban 1998:271)

These issues do not exempt anthropologists' research from ethical review (Fluehr-Lobban 1998), but they do require that ethnographers provide sufficient information to review boards to both identify and defend any alternative procedures that may be required by the culture or the community, or the methods that are embedded in a particular ethnographic study. However, that does not always resolve the problems the IRB poses for social science researchers, particularly those employing grounded theory and/or qualitative and generative methods.

The history of IRBs is dotted with examples of the process called "mission creep" (Lederman 2006b), in which local IRBs evolve into institutional bodies that are primarily concerned with the protection of the institution (especially in a litigious society), rather than protecting the human subject participants in research projects conducted by the institution. As a consequence, anthropologists have found it useful to inform, educate, and negotiate with IRBs about the methods, conditions, and traditions of anthropological research, especially traditions of cultural preservation for future generations, the protection of cultural context, and the necessity of cultural accommodation in ethical issues in ways that meet crosscultural needs of both the IRB and the community being studied.

IRBs are deliberately designed as local (decentralized) ethical review systems, and as a consequence, they can vary significantly on their views of many of the standards and procedures for human subjects protections. This variability, however, is also an opportunity for implementing creative solutions to rules that are problematic, since the decision-making power is in local hands (Katz 2006). The current state of the discussion of IRBs in anthropology from this view of the issue is well summarized by an anthropologist who is not subject to U.S. IRB regulations in her normal research context.

> As practitioners of a discipline that specializes in angst-ridden discussions about ethics and about whether to treat people in the field as human subjects or as interlocutors, key informants, collaborators, or friends, anthropologists, not surprisingly, feel especially resentful and threatened when faced with institutional review board (IRB) procedures. As a working anthropologist reading the articles in this AE Forum, I could instantly empathize with Rena Lederman's indignation about being forced to translate the disciplinary assumptions and protocols of other subjects to anthropology; the helplessness that some contributors (e.g., Jack Katz and Daniel Bradburd) express in deciding when a research moment begins and ordinary life leaves off; and the sheer puzzlement of how one might be expected to get prior informed consent, when participant-observation is all about entering into the contexts of other people's lives.

As someone based outside the United States, I find it difficult to assess how much anthropological research is really blocked by IRBs and how far the sense of siege these articles convey is shared across universities. An unscientific e-mail survey I conducted of colleagues (mostly anthropologists, but not all) at different U.S. universities showed that everyone has had something to do with IRBs but the way they have been affected has varied. Whereas the finer points of federal mission creep into non–federally funded projects, the scope of exemptions clauses, or the need to rewrite IRB rules to allow for the differing methodologies of different disciplines are clearly issues for U.S. anthropologists and university administrators to debate; from my vantage point, it seems more important that the notion of "consent" itself be problematized and not just the manner of its procurement. Some requirement that people, whether communities or individuals, be informed of the goals of research is not unreasonable. Coming from a national context in which the power of anthropology to represent people is limited, research funding and consequent oversight are negligible, and questions of consent are rarely debated, I think something like an IRB might not be a bad idea. At least, these issues would get raised in the consciousness of researchers. (Sundar 2006:535–536)

## AMERICAN ANTHROPOLOGY AND ETHICS

In chapter 1 we referenced the man often referred to as the father of American anthropology—Franz Boas—and his public denunciation of anthropologists who acted as spies. Boas' letter that was published in *The Nation* decried the use of anthropologists to provide information about subject people to governments. While Boas' outrage is a welcome antidote to the complacent acceptance of anthropological data being used to control native peoples, it was hardly a novel activity. Early ethnographers were frequently employed by their colonial governments to learn about the people such governments were trying to subdue; some government agents actually became ethnographers in the process. We may think of those employed by the British Foreign Service as examples of these early ethnographers (Evans-Pritchard among others), but some American anthropologists also actively conducted research for the government.

Anthropological involvement became more present and more visible following the U.S. entry into World War II. By 1941, a committee had been formed to assist in the war effort by mobilizing scholars from the behavioral sciences to work on topics such as psychological warfare and morale. The Committee for National Morale (CNM) received contributions from such well-known anthropologists as Gregory Bateson, Margaret Mead, Ruth Benedict, and Geoffrey Gorer (Fluehr-Lobban

2003). By the end of World War II, approximately half the anthropologists in the U.S. had contributed to the war effort, many of them working for the Office of Strategic Service (OSS), military intelligence, and the Office of War Information (Fluehr-Lobban 2003; Price 2000).

Following the end of the war, the OSS became the CIA and still had need for trained anthropologists to work for them in secret (Fluehr-Lobban 2003; Price 2000). The role of secret research became an issue in anthropology that would not go away. Simultaneously, applied research activities grew. In 1941, the Society for Applied Anthropology was formed by a multidisciplinary group of social scientists (Whiteford 2004) whose aim was to translate anthropological ideas about social organization and human and industrial relations to improving life and solving social problems. Many of the younger members of the society did research on private industries (one of the most famous was the Western Hawthorne Electric Study, in which researchers interviewed 21,000 employees to evaluate influences on productivity) and government (on topics such as race relations). The public acknowledgement of the use of anthropological research stimulated the SfAA to create the first anthropological statement on professional ethics in 1948. It was also one of the first in the social sciences (Fluehr-Lobban 2003; Whiteford 2004).

It was the role of anthropologists in the war in Vietnam and Project Camelot that really brought the discussion of anthropological ethics into focus and resulted in the creation of the first Statement on Problems of Anthropological Research and Ethics by the AAA in 1967. Project Camelot came from the Department of the Army's Office of the Chief of Research and Development. The aim of the project was a "basic social science research project on preconditions of internal conflict and on effects of indigenous governmental actions—easing, exacerbating, or resolving—of those conditions" (Sjoberg 1967:142 in Fluehr-Lobban 2003:8). The point of the research was for the army to learn how to control and remove the growing number of resistance movements, particularly those in Latin America. By the time the project ended because of public outrage, many social scientists—primarily sociologists and psychologists, not anthropologists—had been hired (Fluehr-Lobban 2003:8).

Regardless of the role of anthropologists in Project Camelot, the experience embittered Latin American anthropologists, made any research in Latin America by a U.S. researcher suspect, focused concern about government funding for anthropological research, and raised the issue of secret research. At the 1966 meeting of the AAA, those attending adopted a resolution calling for the executive board "to explore the widely ramified issues involving the relationship between anthropologists and the agencies, both governmental and private, that sponsor their research" (*Anthropology Newsletter* 1966:1–2,

in Fluehr-Lobban 2003:9) The statements on ethics from both SfAA
and AAA reaffirm the anthropological obligations to do no harm to
those they study, to science, to society, or to fellow researchers.

The next crisis, however, was truly a crucible for the discipline.
The Department of Defense placed an ad in the August 1968 issue of
the *American Anthropologist* for an anthropologist to "work with the
Psychological Operations Headquarters in Vietnam. Duties included
research, analysis, and interpretations of findings relative to the effec-
tiveness of 'enemy' propaganda and U.S. counterpropaganda on 'target
audiences,' and the evaluation of current and proposed psychological
operations" (Fluehr-Lobban 2003:11). Anthropologists were outraged;
the duties clearly would be in contradiction to the AAA 1967 statement against anthropological involvement with clandestine activities.
The ad was withdrawn, but it became clear that there had been, and
continued to be, a clandestine relationship between agencies such as
the CIA and the U.S. military with anthropologists.

In the midst of growing antiwar activities in the United States,
documents were taken from a private campus office that gave evidence of anthropological involvement in the expanding war in Thailand. Those documents were given to Eric Wolf, the chair of the AAA's
Committee on Ethics and also, by some means, were simultaneously
distributed publicly. The political climate was extremely tense and
Wolf was caught in a highly polarized and angry situation. He, along
with another member of the Ethics Committee, were blamed by the
AAA Executive Committee for allowing the information to be made
public and therefore violating their obligations to the Ethics Committee. This is powerfully reminiscent of the professional association that
preceded the AAA (the Washington Anthropological Society) and its
censure of Boas.

It is a dilemma that professional associations like the SfAA and
AAA face—how to respect the right of their members to make employment choices while simultaneously respecting the goals articulated in
their ethical codes and ethical and professional responsibilities. The
development of such codes and the provision of standing committees
on ethics and social justice are, we believe, a crucial step in the movement toward an ethical practice of anthropology. We also believe that
open, public, and fair discussions of existing and developing issues in
the discipline are necessary for a human subjects-based discipline.
Anthropology is not only based on the study of humans, but also often
focuses on the most vulnerable sectors of a population, thus requiring
ongoing discussions of the evolving ethical problems anthropologists
encounter. The many and vivid discussions following the publication of
the *Darkness in El Dorado,* we believe, contributed to important
reflections on what doing research means and on the responsibilities
and obligations we have to studied populations.

Ethics are dynamic, and the situations that give rise to ethical quandaries are constantly changing. Yet there clearly are recurring themes. Protection of our study partners—be they individuals in a clinical study, members of a community, an organization providing services, our colleagues, or the discipline—is a constant obligation. And, as Boas wrote nearly 90 years ago, so is our obligation to doing good science where our methods, sponsorship, and results are transparent and not clandestine. At the time of this writing, the issue of the role of anthropologists in yet another U.S. war is being called into question. Sadly, sociopolitical crises and military actions continue to be enacted on vulnerable populations, making it even more critical for us as members of the discipline to create an ethical practice.

Even a brief and incomplete exploration of the history of legal, moral, and ethical systems provides an important framework for understanding both the content and the dynamics of anthropological research ethics. The anthropological principle of cultural relativism requires that ethical guidelines, actions, and principles be viewed not only within their specific ethical context but also in comparison with other, often-competing, cultural and ethical environments at local and crosscultural levels. Many basic ethical principles have remained prominent and relatively stable through time, but there have been significant changes in the interpretation and the application of those principles: from reciprocal punishment to distributive justice, from sacred to secular interpretations, and from authoritarian to egalitarian frameworks for the justification of those ethical principles.

## Thought Questions

1. One of the key points in this chapter is that ethical rules (laws, customs, and moral premises) reflect the culture that produces them. Construct a table that has five of the laws from the Code of Hammurabi on one side, and five corresponding (similar subject) laws from either federal or from state laws on the other side.

   • What are the primary cultural differences between each of the contrasting (or corresponding) pairs of laws?
   • What overall similarities exist between the two legal systems?

2. What is the difference between ethics, laws, and religious proscriptions?

3. This chapter demonstrates there is a historical and current conflation of ideas and principles that blends religion, civil and secular ethical codes, and the ideas of law.

   • How have secular and sacred ethical principles been combined in either national or international ethical guidelines for research?
   • Which crosscultural stance can you best defend: (a) that cultural relativism means that secular and sacred ethical principles should

be been combined in ethical guidelines for research, and that all researchers should be forced to adhere to the local religious and civil precepts (regardless of their own values), or (b) should cultural relativism mean that cultural groups can be forced to abandon religious precepts in favor of consensus statements about secular research ethics that take the religious precepts into account, but remove the religious sanctions from the process?

- Should ethical principles be more "universal" (one size fits all), or more culturally and situationally relative (everyone has a different set of ethics that have to be accommodated)?
- Who should be the final decision makers on these questions (communities, cultural representatives, researchers, governments)?

4. Pharmaceutical companies spend a considerable amount of money, time, and their workers' energy on the research and development of new drugs. Before these drugs can be marketed to the general public, they go through a number a phases of testing, first on animals and later on humans. In the past, governments have tested these new drugs on soldiers, prisoners, and other captive groups. When this became illegal, the testing moved to vulnerable and often impoverished members of the population. Today, much of the clinical trials for new drugs takes place outside of the U.S.

- Should those populations be protected also?
- Is there any alternative to using money with very poor people as an incentive to their participation?
- Is there anything wrong with paying very vulnerable groups to be experimented on?
- Is participation really voluntary under such circumstances?

## Ethical Dilemma: Female Genital Cutting

People are always fascinated by ideas, beliefs, and behaviors different from their own. For many people in the West, female genital cutting (FGC)—also referred to as female circumcision and genital mutilation—is difficult to understand. It also provides an excellent example for a discussion of ethical issues surrounding responses to a culturally embedded practice that is seen as both moral and desirable within some cultural contexts, and seen as an inhumane violation of individual autonomy and as mutilation in other cultural contexts. The practice has widespread acceptance, is used in many parts of the world, and is often justified with reference to religious beliefs.

Where FGC is a common practice, many women consider it a desirable operation because without it the woman may be considered unmarriageable or ritually "unclean." The FGC process transforms her into a cultural category of "clean and desirable."

Many of the basic human rights embedded in U.S. national laws are present in international law, and are present in international ethical guidelines. However, there are also significant variations and some key differences that are produced by the accommodation of crosscultural differences in the international community. Some of the U.S. and European principles are in conflict with, or at least differ in application, from religious and ideologically based ethical principles in other parts of the world. This creates complications for both the definition, and the application, of universal or international ethical guidelines protecting human subjects in all cultures and for all conditions. There is ongoing debate over the appropriate wording, application, and enforcement of research ethics and research guidelines at the international level. Some countries have adopted the stance that their specific laws and regulations must be met, regardless of crosscultural differences, while others have determined that conflicting guidelines must be resolved to fit both cultures involved.

- What might be the role of the anthropologist as it relates to immigrant populations in the U.S. who desire to continue the practice, as well as those who seek asylum to avoid it?
- How might Western thoughts, ideas, and practices influence each student's personal opinion on the topic?
- What should be the role of medical practitioners in the U.S. who are either asked to perform the procedure or reverse it? How may ethnocentrism or cultural relativism influence this role?
- How should women's advocates deal with the issue of subalternity?
- How should anthropologists address power issues at differing levels (local community, family, etc.)?

### *Recommended Resource Material*

Soraya, Mire. 1994. *Fire Eyes* (video). New York: Filmmakers Library.
Kratz, Corinne A. 2003. Circumcision, pluralism, and dilemmas of cultural relativism. In *Applying Anthropology: An Introductory Reader*, 7th ed., ed. Aaron Podelefsky and Peter J. Brown. Boston: McGraw-Hill, pp. 255–266.

Kate Brelsford developed this case.

*Chapter Three*

---

# Principles for
# Ethical Research

---

The cultural theory embedded in anthropology creates frequent ethical conundrums for anthropologists in general, and for ethnographers in particular (Comitas 2000). Two basic crosscultural issues are at the root of these dilemmas. One is based on the need to respect the principle of cultural relativism—that there are no universal standards by which all cultures may be evaluated. The second issue stems from the need to contextualize judgments of culturally shaped beliefs and behaviors, since those judgments are closely dependent on the perspective of the individual culture. These two principles are axiomatic for conducting sound ethnographic research and practice. Consequently, anthropologists find themselves invested in defending the particular ethics of a single culture against the imposition of either universal ethics or the specific ethics of another culture. Other disciplines—those without adherence to the concept of cultural relativism—tend to see a greater need for a more universalistic approach to ethics. Even when the importance of cultural relativism is acknowledged, however, there is also considerable cross-disciplinary agreement that cultural relativism cannot be ethically extended to all human behavior just because that behavior is strongly endorsed by a specific culture. Nagengast (2004) and other anthropologists have referred to this argument as "blaming culture" for abuses. This is particularly visible in the justifications for cases of infringement of human rights when the argument is made "but it is the way their culture does it."

All cultures recognize that certain behaviors are not acceptable, based on the ideals, mores, and values of their specific culture, and to

some extent, to all human cultures in general. There is a clear historical trend across cultures to restrict and attempt to prevent behaviors
that are considered harmful. These shared perspectives can be viewed
as ethical universals or as consensus ethical principles that are internationally and crossculturally enforced. One of the consensus documents that support this universalistic approach is the United Nations'
Declaration of Universal Human Rights. Another powerful trend in
the same direction is the striking history of national and international
agreements, conventions, and treaties that define, describe, and provide standardized guidelines for crosscultural research and practice
efforts. Those documents, and the principles behind them, are
designed to protect humans from harmful research or harmful practices in professions that focus on human needs and conditions (e.g.,
health, education, or subsistence) as well as from abuses from political
force such as genocide.

     This chapter provides a summary of the ethical principles that
are both nationally and internationally endorsed and regulated in
relation to the ethical conduct of research and the preservation of critical human rights. The chapter also provides a basic model of the ways
in which ethnographic research can accommodate these principles
while remaining sensitive to crosscultural conditions that challenge
some of those principles on a local level, thus resolving the anthropological dilemmas.

## THE BASIC PRINCIPLES

     The basic principles for ethical research have been established
and agreed on both in national governments and by international
treaties around the world. These principles, enforced by sanctions,
also are appropriate guidelines for the practice of anthropology outside of research settings. It is worthwhile to note that when the more
culturally specific national guidelines are compared with the more
generic international guidelines that take into account a much wider
cultural, legal, philosophical, religious, and ethical spectrum, important differences are especially visible. Nevertheless, three well-estab-
lished principles are considered the standard foundation for the
ethical treatment of people in human research as well as in anthropological practice. In the United States, these were first clearly defined
in The Belmont Report and then refined through time and case experience. These principles are: (1) respect for persons, (2) maximize good
for people and minimize harm, and (3) insure basic social justice for
people participating in human research. Understanding these principles allows anthropologists to design, conduct, and evaluate their own

and other anthropologists' adherence to the basic Principles of Professional Conduct and the current ethical guidelines for the discipline.

## Respect for Persons

The first principle—respect for persons—is primarily directed at protecting individual human rights over the rights of a society or government by assuring that individuals (not authorities or others) have the right to choose whether or not they want to (or should) participate in research. Participation should be under individual control, not under the control of some other person or entity. The following definitions of this principle and its corollaries are provided below:

**Respect for Persons.** Respect for persons incorporates at least two ethical convictions: first, that individuals should be treated as autonomous agents, and second, that persons with diminished autonomy are entitled to protection. The principle of respect for persons thus divides into two separate moral requirements: the requirement to acknowledge autonomy and the requirement to protect those with diminished autonomy.

An autonomous person is an individual capable of deliberation about personal goals and of acting under the direction of such deliberation. To respect autonomy is to give weight to autonomous persons' considered opinions and choices while refraining from obstructing their actions unless they are clearly detrimental to others. To show lack of respect for an autonomous agent is to repudiate that person's considered judgments, to deny an individual the freedom to act on those considered judgments, or to withhold information necessary to make a considered judgment, when there are no compelling reasons to do so.

However, not every human being is capable of self-determination. The capacity for self-determination matures during an individual's life, and some individuals lose this capacity wholly or in part because of illness, mental disability, or circumstances that severely restrict liberty. Respect for the immature and the incapacitated may require protecting them as they mature or while they are incapacitated.

Some persons are in need of extensive protection, even to the point of excluding them from activities which may harm them; other persons require little protection beyond making sure they undertake activities freely and with awareness of possible adverse consequence. The extent of protection afforded should depend upon the risk of harm and the likelihood of benefit. The judgment that any individual lacks autonomy should be periodically reevaluated and will vary in different situations.

In most cases of research involving human subjects, respect for persons demands that subjects enter into the research voluntarily and with adequate information. In some situations, however, application of the principle is not obvious. The involvement of prisoners as subjects of research provides an instructive example. On the one hand, it would seem that the principle of respect for persons requires that prisoners not be deprived of the opportunity to volunteer for research. On the other hand, under prison conditions they may be subtly coerced or unduly influenced to engage in research activities for which they would not otherwise volunteer. Respect for persons would then dictate that prisoners be protected. Whether to allow prisoners to "volunteer" or to "protect" them presents a dilemma. Respecting persons, in most hard cases, is often a matter of balancing competing claims urged by the principle of respect itself. (The Belmont Report 1979, Part B: Basic Ethical Principles)

The concept of respect for persons is central to Western philosophical thought, which emphasizes the rights and the obligations of the individual rather than those of groups or society as a whole. The principle of respect for persons has two primary components. The first is a belief in *individual autonomy*. The second is a belief in *free will* and *self-determination*. Individual autonomy encompasses the ideal that each person has the right to make his or her own decisions and the obligation to accept the consequences of those decisions. Each person has the right to be autonomous, rather than being controlled by others or by social forces. The concept of free will is the belief that individuals are free to make decisions according to their own conscience (beliefs and values), without interference from destiny or from external secular, supernatural, or political pressure. Free will produces the opportunity for self-determination—one's ability to determine his or her own future or actions, rather than having those actions determined by an outside authority or authorities, including a government that uses some form of coercion.

These principles are among the primary philosophical foundations for many of the values, laws, and freedoms people are theoretically guaranteed in U.S. culture. The founders of the United States Constitution acknowledged these three principles in the Declaration of Independence and codified them in the Bill of Rights. The Bill of Rights is, therefore, a key foundational document for establishing ethical research principles within the United States, especially in those cases where the rights of the individual are challenged by the government or a religious organization by means of coercion or persecution (Amar 1998).

The concept of autonomy, however, and the cultural differences around the world in people's understanding of respect for persons, also produce some important challenges for anthropologists conducting ethical research. Autonomy is a concept that is present in many but not necessarily all cultures, and the level of autonomy allowed by that culture (as opposed to group-level imposition of norms and actions) varies widely—as do the beliefs about for whom and by whom autonomy should be granted. These differences in beliefs about autonomy often become codified into restrictions that may have negative consequences for particular groups of people—the poor, women, and other socially marginalized people. Internationally, both respect for persons and the concept of justice are embedded in the United Nations' Declaration of Universal Human Rights (Morsink 2000; Symonides 2000), but both concepts show wide variations in the local, culturally imposed definitions of respect, beneficence, and justice.

## Beneficence (Do No Harm)

The principle of beneficence was first embedded in medical and health research, and then extended to social research. Beneficence requires researchers to do more good than harm—to improve both society and individuals' lives. Research is considered a common good and researchers are required to either avoid or minimize any harm that might be caused by the research. The Belmont Report establishes two complementary principles that must be applied to individuals who are participating in research projects. The first principle is do no harm. This principle reflects the medical research roots for many of the principles and the procedures for conducting ethical research on human subjects. The concept of doing no harm is philosophically tied to the Hippocratic Oath that physicians used to take in the twentieth century, in which they vowed to work to the best of their knowledge and abilities; if they could not help, then at least they would do no harm. The incorporation of this principle into medical oaths is also a direct result from the harm that was caused by unethical human experimentation early in the twentieth century.

The Belmont Report and many other research ethics guidelines also acknowledge that the fundamental principle of doing absolutely no harm is sometimes impossible to achieve. As a consequence, for some research, conditions where the natural or unimpeded outcome of some situation or condition is "great harm," researchers are allowed to cause or to allow some level of harm to occur as a result of their research if the research has the clear potential to produce more benefit than harm. This situation, however, can be a very slippery slope and one in which the review of an external group such as an IRB can be both insightful and necessary. This second complementary principle from The Belmont Report can be stated as: maximize benefits and minimize harms. In either case, it requires that the researcher engage in an assessment of both the risks and benefits of the research. The following excerpt from The Belmont Report frames the important conditions that revolve around the commitment to the common good that researchers make when conducting research ethically.

> **Beneficence.** Persons are treated in an ethical manner not only by respecting their decisions and protecting them from harm, but also by making efforts to secure their well-being. Such treatment

falls under the principle of beneficence. The term "beneficence" is often understood to cover acts of kindness or charity that go beyond strict obligation. In this document, beneficence is understood in a stronger sense, as an obligation. Two general rules have been formulated as complementary expressions of beneficent actions in this sense: (1) do not harm and (2) maximize possible benefits and minimize possible harms.

The Hippocratic maxim "do no harm" has long been a fundamental principle of medical ethics. Claude Bernard extended it to the realm of research, saying that one should not injure one person regardless of the benefits that might come to others. However, even avoiding harm requires learning what is harmful; and, in the process of obtaining this information, persons may be exposed to risk of harm. Further, the Hippocratic Oath requires physicians to benefit their patients "according to their best judgment." Learning what will in fact benefit may require exposing persons to risk. The problem posed by these imperatives is to decide when it is justifiable to seek certain benefits despite the risks involved, and when the benefits should be foregone because of the risks.

The obligations of beneficence affect both individual investigators and society at large, because they extend both to particular research projects and to the entire enterprise of research. In the case of particular projects, investigators and members of their institutions are obliged to give forethought to the maximization of benefits and the reduction of risk that might occur from the research investigation. In the case of scientific research in general, members of the larger society are obliged to recognize the longer term benefits and risks that may result from the improvement of knowledge and from the development of novel medical, psychotherapeutic, and social procedures.

The principle of beneficence often occupies a well-defined justifying role in many areas of research involving human subjects. An example is found in research involving children. Effective ways of treating childhood diseases and fostering healthy development are benefits that serve to justify research involving children—even when individual research subjects are not direct beneficiaries. Research also makes it possible to avoid the harm that may result from the application of previously accepted routine practices that on closer investigation turn out to be dangerous. But the role of the principle of beneficence is not always so unambiguous. A difficult ethical problem remains, for example, about research that presents more than minimal risk without immediate prospect of direct benefit to the children involved. Some have argued that such research is inadmissible, while others have pointed out that this limit would rule out much research promising great benefit to children in the future. Here again, as with all hard cases, the different claims covered by the principle of beneficence may come into conflict and force difficult choices. (The Belmont Report 1979, Part B: Basic Ethical Principles)

One example of how the principle transforms from "do no harm" to "minimize harm and maximize benefits" involves research on different kinds of medicines for deadly diseases, such as cancer. Many cancer treatments (surgery, chemotherapy) cause some harm, sometimes even death. If nothing is done for the patient, however, he or she will definitely die. This sets up a situation in which some harm is allowable if the patient agrees and if the benefit outweighs the harm from a big-picture perspective. Cancer research has shown that many of the medicines that are effective against cancer have harmful side effects. Those side effects vary among individuals, but are more acceptable than death for most patients even though they include some temporary or permanent harm. The ethical experimentation to find these drugs is required to take into account the level of harm produced by the treatments, compared with the absolute harm of the disease, and balance the harms against the benefits. The same form of risk analysis is required for sociocultural research, but the configuration of harm to be considered is to the individual, the community, and the society and may take different forms. The principle of respect for persons allows individuals (based on informed consent) to take part in potentially risky and harmful research as long as they voluntarily give their consent (autonomy) and as long as the principle of beneficence (maximize benefits and minimize harm) has been applied to the overall research projects and its potential results.

The research does not have to guarantee positive results, but it has to show a clear potential for positive results. Some of the discussions below show how anthropologists have both supported the principle of beneficence in their research ethics guidelines and praxis and also attacked these very principles. Withdrawing support for beneficence stems from critiques of the field of bioethics, since bioethics is the principal U.S. philosophical tradition that has supported a rules- / principles-based approach to ethical protection of human subjects that some anthropologists find objectionable and biased (Frank et al. 1998; Koenig and Hogle 1995).

## Justice

Human research must be conducted in a way that protects people's right to fair and equitable treatment, a central component of the principle of justice. Many of the protections for fair and equitable treatment are directed at individuals who are members of specific populations and may require special protection because of that membership, rather than needing protection because of their individual characteristics beyond that group membership. The principle of justice is critical for protecting vulnerable populations from the kind of research that was conducted by Josef Mengele and other unethical researchers who have biased ethnic, religious, gender, economic, or political views and agendas (Penslar 1995; Rachels and Rachels 2006). It is also the principle that requires that no group of people should be exposed to the risks of research if their group will not also benefit from the research. Others can benefit as well, but there should not be an unjust level of risk for some groups and an unjust reward for others. The Belmont Report makes justice a clear requirement for ethical research. And while The Belmont Report was aimed to protect human subjects in medical research, the same principle applies in anthropological practice.

> **Justice.** Who ought to receive the benefits of research and bear its burdens? This is a question of justice, in the sense of "fairness in distribution" or "what is deserved." An injustice occurs when some benefit to which a person is entitled is denied without good reason or when some burden is imposed unduly. Another way of conceiving the principle of justice is that equals ought to be treated equally. However, this statement requires explication. Who is equal and who is unequal? What considerations justify departure from equal distribution? Almost all commentators allow that distinctions based on experience, age, deprivation, competence, merit and position do sometimes constitute criteria justifying differential treatment for certain purposes. It is necessary, then, to explain in what respects people should be treated equally. There are several widely accepted formulations of just ways to distribute burdens and benefits. Each formulation mentions some relevant property on the basis of which burdens and benefits should be distributed. These formulations are (1) to each person an equal share, (2) to each person according to individual need, (3) to each person according to individual effort, (4) to each person according to societal contribution, and (5) to each person according to merit.
>
> Questions of justice have long been associated with social practices such as punishment, taxation and political representation. Until recently these questions have not generally been associated with scientific research. However, they are foreshadowed even in the earliest reflections on the ethics of research involving human subjects. For example, during the 19th and early 20th centuries the burdens of serving as research subjects fell largely upon poor ward patients, while the benefits of improved medical care flowed primarily to private patients. Subsequently, the exploitation of unwilling prisoners as research subjects in Nazi concentration camps was condemned as a particularly flagrant injustice. In this country, in the 1940s, the Tuskegee syphilis study used disadvantaged, rural black men to study the untreated course of a disease that is by no means confined to that population. These subjects were deprived of demonstrably effective treatment in order not to interrupt the project, long after such treatment became generally available.
>
> Against this historical background, it can be seen how conceptions of justice are relevant to research involving human subjects. For example, the selection of research subjects needs to be scrutinized in order to determine whether some classes (e.g., welfare

patients, particular racial and ethnic minorities, or persons con-
fined to institutions) are being systematically selected simply
because of their easy availability, their compromised position, or
their manipulability, rather than for reasons directly related to the
problem being studied. Finally, whenever research supported by
public funds leads to the development of therapeutic devices and
procedures, justice demands both that these not provide advantages only to those who can afford them and that such research should
not unduly involve persons from groups unlikely to be among the
beneficiaries of subsequent applications of the research. (The Belmont Report 1979, Part B: Basic Ethical Principles)

## THE RIGHT TO PRIVACY AND OTHER BASIC CIVIL RIGHTS

There are two U.S. laws that have a direct and essential impact
on the way in which ethical principles for human research are defined
and understood: (1) privacy and confidentiality and (2) civil rights.
The privacy laws establish a right for people to protect themselves
from having private and potentially harmful information about themselves disclosed to anyone (individuals or institutions) who have no
right to access to the information. Privacy is a fairly recent cultural
concept in Western cultures. It is the belief that each individual has
the right to keep highly personal information from other people (principle of privacy) because it may be harmful (socially, financially, or
physically) if other people know it. If the information has to be shared
(for example in a research project), then each person has the right to
have every possible effort taken to protect that information from fall-
ing into the hands of anyone who is not authorized to have access to it
(principle of confidentiality). The legal definitions and precedents for
privacy and confidentiality are found in the Privacy Act of 1974 and in
its subsequent revisions. This law strongly supports the processes that
are embedded in the principle of respect for persons described below.

### What Is the Difference between Privacy and Confidentiality?

- Confidentiality pertains to data. Confidentiality means making
  sure others don't have more access to information about you
  than you want them to have.
- Privacy pertains to people. Privacy means making sure others
  don't have more access to you than you want them to have. (East
  Tennessee State University: http://www.etsu.edu/irb/privacy%
  20presentation.pdf, citing 45 CFR-46.111)
- Privacy is about persons and their sense of being in control of
  the access of others to themselves. (Sieber J., Procedures to Pro-

tect Privacy and Maintain Confidentiality, California State University:     http://www.aascu.org/ofpopen/ohrp05/MeetMaterial/PrivacyConfidentiality.pdf)

The U.S. Civil Rights Act of 1964 is the second crucial law that directly relates to research ethics in the United States. The law provides a legal guarantee of a number of rights that are directly tied to the ways that research ethics guidelines are constructed and interpreted in the United States, based on the ethical principle of justice (as well as protection of property rights, access to due process, and access to equal treatment under the law). The law prohibits researchers from allowing people to become the victims of discrimination on the basis of race, gender, religion, economic status, or other civil conditions in their participation in research. These principles are also defined—internationally and crossculturally—in the United Nations' Universal Declaration of Human Rights (Morsink 2000).

The basic principles for ethical research, along with the basic civil rights of U.S. citizens and their legal rights for the protection of their own privacy, their property (including intellectual property), and their selves from intrusion, discrimination, or other forms of harm, are the primary framework for anthropological research ethics and relevant for both research and practice. These principles and laws are subject to interpretation, debate, challenge, and revision, but they are also subject to enforcement.

## Thought Questions

1. Can you think of any additional principles for ethical conduct of research beyond the current three (respect for persons, beneficence, and justice) that would be accepted crossculturally to shape international research ethics guidelines?

2. The three primary principles guiding research ethics have been defined and have been elaborated on for more than fifty years.
   - Are there any other higher (summative) principles that you feel should be added, or are the principles that others are proposing subcategories within these three?
   - Should any of the three principles be eliminated?
   - Are the basic elements of the principles (autonomy, minimize harm, maximize benefit, fairness, equity) sufficient for producing ethical research for the future?

3. Can you think of crosscultural situations in which these principles may not apply? For instance, do all societies define the concept of privacy in the same way?
   - Do people living in a small, rural town in the U.S. have the same concept of privacy as do people in a large, urban city?

- Do people in other cultures—a culture other than your own— show respect in the same way?
- If they do not, how can we effect the concept of respect for persons in crosscultural research or practice?

## Ethical Dilemma: Moral Judgment in Alto do Cruzeiro

The scenario below illustrates the tendency for some anthropologists to decide to override the concept of cultural relativism when that concept is in conflict with their own moral judgment; consequently, they carry out an activity that is not requested or advocated (or approved of) by at least part of the community they are studying.

*Death Without Weeping* describes Nancy Scheper-Hughes' fieldwork in Alto do Cruzeiro, a Brazilian shantytown. In the ethnography, she takes a severely malnourished child from his home and force feeds him back to health before returning him to his family.

- Are Scheper-Hughes' actions "moral"?
- Are "moral actions" justified by the basic ethics principles embedded in the Nuremberg Accord, the Belmont Report, or the Helsinki Accords? If so, how do these universalist principles trump the universalist principle of cultural relativism? If not, why not?

Anthropologists frequently engage in long-term research in which they return to a single community or research population over a period of years. Often they create close and abiding relations with the people in that community, becoming godparents to children of friends in the community, lending help when it is needed, protecting their interests when called on.

- Does that kind of relationship improve the research results?
- Does that kind of relationship compromise the research process?
- Does research need to be conducted in the absence of personal relationships in order to be scientific?
- Do personal relationships in research settings deepen the researcher's knowledge?

In general, does anthropology:

- Combat ethnocentrism?
- Support human rights?
- Promote cultural relativism?
- What are some of the tensions in competing (universal standards and cultural relativism) anthropological concepts?
- Does cultural relativism preclude anthropological support for human rights?
- On what anthropological basis can human rights be defended?

### Recommended Resource Material

Cassidy, C. M. 1987. World-view conflict and toddler malnutrition: Change agent dilemmas. In *Child Survival,* ed. Nancy Scheper-Hughes, pp. 293–324. New York: Springer.

Hastrupp, K. and P. Elsass.1990 Anthropological advocacy: A contradiction in terms? *Anthropology* 31(3):301–311.

Scheper-Hughes, Nancy. 1993. *Death without weeping: The violence of everyday life in Brazil.* Berkeley and Los Angeles: University of California Press.

This case was developed based on ideas from Kate Brelsford, Elizabeth Cooper, Jason Miller, and Marc Hébert.

*Chapter Four*

---

# Respect for Persons

---

The concept of respect for persons includes three guiding conditions—respect for individual autonomy, free will, and self-determination—that establish four basic actions that researchers must accomplish when they conduct ethical research: (1) assuring that participation is voluntary (voluntary participation), (2) determining that individuals recruited into the project are competent to participate (competence), (3) preserving confidentiality for participants (confidentiality), and (4) providing a thorough and accurate informed consent process (informed consent).

---

## VOLUNTARY PARTICIPATION

---

Contemporary anthropological practice reinforces the principle of noncoercive recruitment and participation in human subjects research, which the Nuremberg Code established. Whether for clinical research or community-based applications, the concept of being freely—or as freely as possible—able to choose to participate or to refuse to participate in a project is central to anthropological practice. For this reason, careful consideration must be given to offering incentives for participation, be they remunerative or based on exchange. This can be a delicate problem since anthropologists typically want to recognize the value of time given by those people who choose to work with them or spend time being interviewed by them. That recognition carries with it some expectation of a reward for participants' time; however, among many anthropologists, there is a concern that financial rewards can serve as an irresistible—and therefore, coercive—carrot, unduly influencing people to participate when they otherwise might not. This is most clearly articulated in the many anthropological discussions about large pharmaceutical companies conducting clinical trials in countries where people who have no or small incomes are paid to "volunteer" to participate in the trials. Researchers might come up with alternatives to paying individuals, such as a fieldworker in small rural town making a gift to the community, in which everyone can share. While this does not reward individual participants, gifts of supplies to the local school, health clinic, or other community-based centers are enjoyed and appreciated.

The principle of voluntary participation is translated into U.S. law (45 CFR-46), which requires that anyone who is going to participate in a research project be told and clearly understand that he or she is participating in research and participation is voluntary. Researchers must actively demonstrate that no coercion will be allowed, and no adverse consequences will result from an individual deciding either not to participate in the research or to stop his or her participation during the research project. The law, 45 CFR-46, requires critical elements in any research consent process, including a statement of voluntary participation noted below:

> 8) a statement that participation is voluntary, refusal to partici-
> pate will involve no penalty or loss of benefits to which the subject
> is otherwise entitled, and the subject may discontinue participa-
> tion at any time without penalty or loss of benefits to which the
> subject is otherwise entitled. (Code of Federal Regulations. Title
> 45, Part 46. Revised 6/23/05, 46.16, http://www.nihtraining.com/
> ohsrsite/guidelines/45Cfr46.html#subparta)

The minimum application of this principle is to carefully assess whether or not participation is voluntary by critically reviewing: (1) the process that was used to recruit people into the research project, (2) the process of informed consent before and during participation, and (3) the discussions of the risks and benefits that are identified for a particular project. If any one of those conditions—or any combination of them—can be considered to create too much social, economic, or moral pressure, or any other type of coercive pressure to participate, then the process or condition must be modified to eliminate the coercion and to fit the ethical guidelines.

Rewards, bribes, or promises may constitute coercion if the participant is vulnerable to compensation. Social pressure is coercion when the pressure would automatically tip the balance in favor of participation in spite of the research subject's reluctance to participate. There are numerous ways to exert coercive pressure. Children can be coerced by having their friends pressure them to participate, by having their parents say they will participate, or by having someone in authority asking them to participate when they think the authority does not give them any choice. Adults can be pressured into participating by being offered rewards (payment for participation, access to services, opportunity to go somewhere or do something they cannot afford on their own) that are more compelling than the actual benefits of the research. People who are institutionalized (in prisons, hospitals, mental institutions) can be coerced by boredom (just the opportunity to do something they do not normally do). Voluntary participation has to be free of both outright coercion and undue social pressure. It must also be free of any deception that might cause them to participate when they would not have participated if the deception was not present. While these protections are agreed on in the abstract, they are more difficult to implement in actual field situations. Institutional Review Boards can be very useful in helping the anthropologist identify potential sources of conflicts.

The use of deception to recruit people into a research project, or as part of the project itself, is also a violation of the principle of voluntary participation. The voluntarism rule is violated if people are deceived about the nature of the research or the nature of their participation, especially when that deception hides or understates the actual risks of the research or overstates the rewards. Some ethical problems in social science research have been created by fuzziness or equivocation in the definitions of deception and the way the rules against deception have been applied by various researchers and different disciplines (Allen 1997; Sieber 1982, 1983). It is useful to recall that the guidelines of both the American Anthropological Association and the Society for Applied Anthropology caution against the use of deception in research and practice.

The ethics review boards and the ethical guidelines of many science disciplines allow some deception to occur in research projects when the value of the research outweighs the type of harm created by the deception involved in the research. The risk-benefit analysis focuses on the benefits and considers the risks to be relatively minor. In other disciplines, virtually no deception is felt to be justified. Much of this variation—and even confusion—regarding the use of deception has been a part of the research ethics debate since its inception. The following excerpt from the Council for International Organizations of Medical Sciences (CIOMS) provides an example of the international discussion of the issue of deception and provides some alternative justifications for and against deception. The CIOMS provides an international forum that adds to the crosscultural debate on research ethics and provides insights into the issues that have created difficulties for researchers in different communities.

**Withholding information and deception.** Sometimes, to ensure the validity of research, investigators withhold certain information in the consent process. In biomedical research, this typically takes the form of withholding information about the purpose of specific procedures. For example, subjects in clinical trials are often not told the purpose of tests performed to monitor their compliance with the protocol, since if they knew their compliance was being monitored they might modify their behavior and hence invalidate results. In most such cases, the prospective subjects are asked to consent to remain uninformed of the purpose of some procedures until the research is completed; after the conclusion of the study they are given the omitted information. In other cases, because a request for permission to withhold some information would jeopardize the validity of the research, subjects are not told that some information has been withheld until the research has been completed. Any such procedure must receive the explicit approval of the ethical review committee.

Active deception of subjects is considerably more controversial than simply withholding certain information. Lying to subjects is a tactic not commonly employed in biomedical research. Social and behavioral scientists, however, sometimes deliberately misinform subjects to study their attitudes and behavior. For example, scientists have pretended to be patients to study the behavior of health-care professionals and patients in their natural settings.

Some people maintain that active deception is never permissible. Others would permit it in certain circumstances. Deception is not permissible, however, in cases in which the deception itself would disguise the possibility of the subject being exposed to more than minimal risk. When deception is deemed indispensable to the methods of a study the investigators must demonstrate to an ethical review committee that no other research method would suffice; that significant advances could result from the research; and that nothing has been withheld that, if divulged, would cause a reasonable person to refuse to participate. The ethical review committee should determine the consequences for the subject of being deceived, and whether and how deceived subjects should be informed of the deception upon completion of the research. Such informing, commonly called "debriefing," ordinarily entails explaining the reasons for the deception. A subject who disapproves of having been deceived should be offered an opportunity to refuse to allow the investigator to use information thus obtained. Investigators and ethical review committees should be aware that deceiving research subjects may wrong them as well as harm them; subjects may resent not having been informed when they learn that they have participated in a study under false pretenses. In some studies there may be justification for deceiving persons other than the subjects by either withholding or disguising elements of information. Such tactics are often proposed, for example, for studies of the abuse of spouses or children. An ethical review committee must review and approve all proposals to deceive persons other than the subjects. Subjects are entitled to prompt and honest answers to their questions; the ethical review committee must determine for each study whether others who are to be deceived are similarly entitled. (International Ethical Guidelines for Biomedical Research Involving Human Subjects, 2002, http:// www.fhi.org/training/fr/retc/pdf_files/cioms.pdf)

The minimum-standard application of this rule is that any deception in a research project (be it community-based or clinical) must be identified and approved by an ethics review board. It must also be identified to the research subject following the data collection, during a full disclosure debriefing, in order to provide the research subject with the opportunity to withdraw his or her participation (and data) from the project. In anthropology, any violation of the general rule (no deception allowed) can create significant problems in defending the ethics of individual research projects and the view of research by the public, since it is often much more difficult to decide how much deception should be allowed, rather than simply deciding that any deception should be automatically forbidden.

The argument made in favor of mild forms of deception is that the "ends justify the means," which has proven to be an ethical slippery slope. The history of anthropology has shown that deception rarely provides sufficient demonstrable scientific advantage to the researcher and, instead, provides disadvantages and negative consequences. Some of the consequences of research/practice employing deceit as a conscious method include loss of credibility as a scientist and loss of access to communities and cultures who justifiably feel they have been deceived. In a litigious society like the United States, it also makes the researcher and research sponsors vulnerable to litigation.

## COMPETENCE TO PARTICIPATE

One of the required actions for ethical research is to include a procedure that assures the participation of only legally and ethically competent individuals. That means that potential participants must be able to understand what they are consenting to. Participants must have the appropriate, culturally defined ability to make their own decisions and have sufficiently mature judgment to understand the consequences of those decisions. Free will and self-determination are effective only when the individual who is supposed to use free will and self-determination has the competence to do so. But free will and self-determination are not enough; researcher/practitioner disclosure in appropriate fashion are equally critical.

U.S. laws and dominant cultural values place limits on who is deemed competent to make appropriate judgments about whether or not to participate in research projects. This is the reason that children and individuals with certain mental conditions are prevented from participating in research unless their legal guardians have reviewed risks and benefits of the research and have given their permission to participate. The competency laws and guidelines recognize certain individuals are either temporarily or permanently unable to make critical decisions. One of the most common competency restrictions is that children are not considered legally competent to decide whether or not to participate in research until they reach of age of 18, or whatever age a particular locality determines. Until then, their parents are required to make that judgment for them. The parents have the right to give consent or to refuse consent to their children's participation. Children are also allowed to express their willingness to participate by giving their assent to participate (they can say yes or no once their parent has said yes), so they are not totally excluded from the rule of voluntary participation. If a child says no, that answer takes precedent over the parent's permission to participate. The situation in which parents give consent for the child but the child refuses is a focal point of a fictional case of using one child as the medical supplier (bone marrow, blood products, etc.) for her sister who is terminally ill (*My Sister's Keeper* by Jodi Picout).

In this time of organ donation, organ harvesting, and high-tech reproductive techniques, these issues are increasingly becoming the focus of anthropological research and practice (Scheper-Hughes 2002; Sharp 2001; Taylor 2004; Tober 2002). This is an area of considerable ethical debate and crosscultural controversy. Cultures differ on the age at which a child is allowed to make decisions for him- or herself. For example, each state in the United States has separate—and often quite different—laws regarding the age of consent for children. These laws define when children are considered competent to make their own decisions and when their parents have the right to make those decisions for them. Concerns about the age at which a child can consent to participate often makes doing crosscultural research problematic. U.S. anthropologists have research concerns about infectious disease distribution among female children married at very young ages in India, or life experiences of adolescent and preadolescent orphan children in Malawi. In order to conduct research on such groups, anthropologists must first convince the IRB in their home institution that these people are competent to consent and that they will be protected from the consequences of such participation.

Likewise, when anthropologists do ethnographic research on street children, they are faced with cultural and legal dilemmas in determining the appropriate individual to give consent for participation in the project. If there are no parents to give consent, can the child give both consent and assent to participate? Where the research is judged to be of minimal risk (that is, it involves the social and psychological risks encountered in everyday life), it may be relatively safe for even very young children to participate. As the risk increases, however, does the age of the child giving assent to participate also need to increase? Since street children's everyday lives involve far more risks than the risks for middle-class children living at home, should the research be designated as minimal risk since it technically fits that definition for these children, or is that an inappropriate designation? In some cultures, children can be emancipated from their parents; children are on their own and/or the parents may be the source of risk and harm rather than a source of protection. Age, knowledge, and maturity are also important. How old, knowledgeable, and mature must a child be to give reasonable informed consent and to make a reasonable judgment about whether or not to participate in research or in an intervention project? The general ethics guidelines are written to protect children from the harm of research in case they cannot understand what they are getting involved in.

Some adults are also judged by law or social convention to be incompetent to exercise free will and self-determination because of a mental condition (from retardation to some forms of mental illness) that interferes with their ability to make sound judgments about their lives, or because they are institutionalized or incarcerated and have legally lost their rights of self-determination for some period of time. The issue of competence has both legal and cultural dimensions that have to be actively addressed in designing ethical research. One area where anthropologists have had to make important situational judgments about competence is in the area of alcohol and drug research.

There are times when it is appropriate to recruit, interview, and observe active alcoholics and drug addicts. Most ethnographers (and ethics review boards) are in agreement that alcohol or drug addicts are competent to consent to participate in research, with the exception of those time periods when they are actively using the substance at a level that obviously impairs their judgment. The primary consequence of that opinion is that the ethnographer has to use his or her judgment for each individual and each situation based on an understanding of the behavior and impairment of the research subject. There are times and circumstances when the ethnographer is ethically required to make the judgment that the person is too impaired to provide informed consent, or to participate in a particular data-collection session, in spite of the stated desire of the participant to participate. This can produce dilemmas for the ethnographer and the research subject that have to be worked out over time. One of the common consequences is that the research subjects become angry over this challenge to their autonomy. They may not only refuse to participate further in the research, but they may also encourage a negative community-level reaction to the research project in general. The flip side to the dilemma is that some individuals may also take advantage of the principle and claim to have been harmed by the research or the data collection because they were too impaired to provide competent informed consent. Either way, the ethnographer may find some guidance through the IRB review and some mechanisms by which to protect him or her and those participating in the project.

## CONFIDENTIALITY

The third action embedded in respect for persons is the protection of confidentiality of the research data provided to the researcher. Ethical confidentiality procedures are designed to protect the information collected in the course of the research. Ideally, such protection will be supported by law to assure that the data will not be used to harm the person socially, financially, or emotionally. This principle requires the researcher to put procedures in place to protect the research data from both accidental and deliberate unauthorized access (Loue 1995).

The right to confidentiality is an extension of the right to privacy. The U.S. Privacy Act of 1974, and its subsequent amendments and expansion within the legal system, define an individual's right to privacy and his or her right to confidentiality. The right to privacy focuses on people's legal rights (and the limits of those rights) to keep anyone outside of the research process from knowing specific kinds of information about them. For example, people have the right not to say anything that might incriminate them when they are suspected of a crime. In the United States, this is considered a fundamental right to privacy; it has resulted in such famous decisions as the *Miranda* decision where criminal suspects have the right not to talk to police.

Privacy rights also are designed to protect people from snooping either by other individuals or by governmental institutions. However, in some cases (e.g., national security concerns), those rights are abrogated. These rights to privacy (limiting the use of wiretaps, listening devices, access to e-mail, etc.) are protections that are both established by the current U.S. legal code and challenged by other parts of the U.S. legal code based on internal and external threats to national security.

The right to confidentiality is a set of laws and legal precedents that place a powerful obligation on the recipient of the confidential information to protect that information from unauthorized access. The person or institution entrusted with the information has to protect it so that others, who should not have access to it, cannot get it and subsequently use it to cause harm. The right to both privacy and confidentiality must be directly and actively protected within the context of any active parts of this protection include protecting people's ... hen they are being recruited into a project, protecting the information they provide, protecting against accidental or deliberate exposure of the information publicly, and protecting people's identities and the information they gave when the research results are being disseminated. But as any fieldworker knows, doing community-based research poses particular problems in trying to protect people's privacy. In a small community where everyone knows each other, people may well be aware of whom the anthropologist interviews, but they should not be able to learn what is said in the interview.

The right to confidentiality and privacy are primarily attached to protecting individuals; however, in anthropology, there is a long tradition of disguising the name and location of the study neighborhood or community in cases where the identification could result in harm to that group. An ethical research design must also take into account the need to protect especially vulnerable groups from harm through the breach of confidentiality. One of the most famous cases of this community/group–level harm occurred early in the HIV/AIDS epidemic when the whole Haitian community in the United States was identified as a risk group. The two other predominant risk groups were identified as homosexuals (men who have sex with men) and injection drug users. Designating the entire Haitian community as a risk group violated all three of the basic principles of ethics. It was a breach of confidentiality that is required in any public health program because it allowed social stigma and harm to be targeted at identifiable individuals regardless of their HIV status. Thus, it was also a violation of the principle of do no harm. Furthermore, it was a violation of justice because it was neither fair nor equitable, and certainly not just. Everyone was put at risk by simply being identified as a member of a community. This was a case where an entire community and culture were stigmatized and harmed, because the general rules of both privacy and confidentiality were breached. That characterization of the Haitian community was later reversed and partially rectified, but not before considerable social harm was done.

## INFORMED CONSENT

The process of informed consent is one of the most important, powerful, and complex actions embedded in the respect for persons section of research/practice ethics. It provides a framework for addressing all of the other actions described above.

Effective communication is vital to participants' comprehension of information during the consent discussion. Misunderstandings and miscommunication are more likely to occur when investigators and participants speak different languages, when informed consent documents must be translated, or when scientific research and the notion of informed consent are unfamiliar to study participants. Recommendations and guidelines for informed consent stress the need for simplicity and clarity. Yet, the language used in consent forms, the amount of information, and their legalistic format may be confusing for someone being asked to join a study in culturally diverse populations throughout the world. (Marshall 2006:25)

The action of informed consent is a doctrine arising from the law of torts. Informed consent is intended to disclose all of the critical elements of a specific research project that individuals need to know in order to make a rational decision to participate in the research project or to decline participation (Faden and Beauchamp 1986).

There has been considerable discussion, debate, and a gradual evolution of the overall understanding of informed consent within anthropological research (cf. Kelly 2003 for an in-depth exploration of the issues). At the present time, there is consensus that the primary informed consent process must be conducted before the individual agrees to participate. This process must be free of social pressure and coercion. The process must clearly explain how confidentiality and privacy will be maintained for both the individual and the data he or she provides. Finally, the process must clearly present to the individual all of the risks and benefits that are associated with the research so that the person can decide whether or not to participate based on his or her own standards. The process must be carefully and specifically constructed to fit the needs and the special circumstances of whoever the research subjects are, including any special needs they may have (e.g., language barriers, mental challenges, physical challenges, etc.). During an extended period of fieldwork, that process must be repeated.

The most common way that the informed consent process is pursued in the United States is through the use of a written informed consent form that is presented to potential research participants as part of the research recruitment process. The general goals and hopes for the project are first presented verbally. If people are interested in participating, the project recruiter then goes over the details of the project that are presented in the informed consent form. The final stage of the informed consent process is to ask the person to sign the consent form, acknowledging that he or she understands the risks and the benefits of the project and that participation is voluntary.

One of the noted ironies of crosscultural research, however, is that in some contexts, having a signed consent form, which is required by IRBs, may present a greater danger than not having the form in the first place (Lederman 2006a:22). Researchers in countries undergoing political strife, or where recent political action has occurred, may find people willing and able to participate because they have important stories to tell and information to share from their experiences; however, they may be reluctant to put their name on any form that might eventually surface and endanger them. People contributing to ethnographic research during the "dirty war" in Argentina (which refers to a period from roughly 1976 to 1983 in which certain groups of citizens were targeted and killed), during and following the civil war in Guatemala (which was the longest civil war in Latin American history, leaving over 200,000 dead), fleeing genocide in the Kosovo/Bosnia conflict (which took place after the breakup of Yugoslavia and resulted in ethnic cleansing), and in many less-dramatic yet still potentially dangerous places where anthropologists work, refused to put their names on paper. Luckily, a verbal consent is an ethical alternative to using a written consent form (Levine1991; Lidz et al. 1983; Marshall 2006) for cultural circumstances where verbal consent (witnessed by the ethnographer) is more appropriate.

Ethnographic research, in particular, encounters circumstances where the need is to follow alternate, but equally valid, procedures rather than relying solely on written language. For example, when ethnographers are working on HIV/AIDS prevention projects with individuals who are engaged in illegal activities (drug use, prostitution), having those individuals sign a consent form creates a confidentially risk if those forms can be accessed by a law enforcement agent, while a verbal informed consent process provides better protection for the participants. The regulations themselves focus on the desired outcome of the process of informed consent, rather than on a specific form (written, verbal, etc.), while some IRBs focus on the form and ignore the impact of that form on the process. Both conditions can be accommodated.

The verbal and/or written informed consent process must both provide and summarize all of the detailed information that is needed to allow the potential research participant to make a voluntary and informed decision to participate or to not participate.

The informed consent process must:

- identify the researchers and the research institution;
- indicate whom to contact for answers to pertinent questions about the research and research subjects' rights; and
- include contact information in the event of a research-related injury to the subject.

Minimally, the following content must also be presented:

- statement that the study involves research and therefore must follow ethical guidelines;
- explanation of the purposes of the research;
- expected duration of the subject's participation;

- description of the procedures to be followed described in a way that is understandable to the participant;
- identification of any procedures that are experimental (untried, new);
- description of any reasonably foreseeable risks or discomforts to the subject;
- description of any benefits to the subject or to others that may reasonably be expected from the research;
- disclosure of appropriate alternative procedures or courses of treatment, if any, that might be advantageous to the subject instead of the research condition;
- statement describing the extent, if any, to which confidentiality of records identifying the subject will be maintained; and, for research involving more than minimal risk (i.e., the risks encountered in everyday life);
- explanation as to whether any compensation will be given;
- explanation as to whether any medical treatments are available if injury occurs and, if so, what they consist of, or where further information may be obtained if the person needs some form of additional help; and
- statement that the subject's refusal to participate will involve no penalty or loss of benefits to which the subject is otherwise entitled and that the subject may discontinue participation at any time without penalty or loss of benefits to which the subject is otherwise entitled.

There are numerous circumstances where the informed consent process has to be culturally adjusted to be effective and ethical. In some cases, the reading level of the consent form must be adjusted. When people are unable to read it, the consent process must be verbal, rather than written, or the consent form must be in the primary language of the research subject. How does the ethnographer translate concepts that are meaningful for him or her, but meaningless for the particular population being interviewed? How, for instance, do you explain the concept of probable odds of a fetus presenting genetic defects to a woman who has no understanding of the terms "probable odds" and "genetic defects"? For that matter, how do you explain "genetics"? Anthropologists Rayna Rapp and Carole Browner, among others, have struggled to understand how to communicate not only across cultures but also across concepts and assumptions.

> The legalistic rendering of consent models used by most IRBs fails to recognize the social construction of informed consent as an act of communication [Kaufert and O'Neil 1990; Kaufert and Putsch 1992; Marta 1996; Kuczewski and Marshall 2001. A number of fac-

tors influence approaches to implementing voluntary informed consent—the nature of the research, the cultural context of the research project, communication issues influencing comprehension of information, and discrepancies in social power between participant and researcher. Yet, underlying assumptions embedded in the western notion of voluntary informed consent are often ignored—assumptions about language and the meanings attached to words and concepts and assumptions about social relationships and the social positioning of individuals within families, institutions, and communities. (Marshall 2003:274)

This process of unpacking informed consent so that it may truly be a process of informing in culturally appropriate ways so that consent (or its refusal) may be based on sufficient information is an intellectually challenging and rewarding endeavor. As long as informed consent is treated as a process to provide individuals with all of the information they need, and all of the opportunity they need to explore and understand the risks they are taking with a particular research project, the project will meet the standards of informed consent.

# ISSUES IN CROSSCULTURAL ETHNOGRAPHIC RESEARCH

Anthropologists and other researchers who conduct research in crosscultural contexts are presented with a complex set of ethical challenges. Researchers need to conduct research that simultaneously accommodates the principles, guidelines, and values of their national culture, of the international community, and of the culture they are studying. They are occasionally caught between the demands of assumed universalism, cultural relativism, and the need to avoid ethnocentric judgments about other cultures. Thus, in order to conduct ethical research, anthropologists have to contend with respect for persons as well as respect for crosscultural variations in the ways in which such concepts as autonomy, free will, and self-determination are understood in various cultures. In spite of the Universal Declaration of Human Rights, these concepts are not universal. For example, some cultures restrict autonomy on the basis of age and gender, or even marital status, with the result that certain individuals might be harmed if they made the choice to participate in research without the permission of someone else in their family, such as a parent or a spouse, giving that permission first, even though those individuals would be considered fully autonomous in the United States.

Just as the concept of autonomy varies among cultures, so does free will. As a consequence, voluntary participation, informed consent, or even the issue of privacy and confidentiality may need additional explanation and even creative accommodation in order for crosscultural researchers to meet the ethical standards of their own society and simultaneously accommodate the ethical standards of the culture they are studying. If one culture views voluntary participation as being based on the willing deference to authority (rather than resistance to authority), and another views voluntary participation as a completely autonomous act and views any statement by authority as coercion, then how can a researcher who is attempting to meet the ethical standards of both cultures do so without violating one of the ethical principles described above? The same question holds for the issue of competence, where the definition of who is competent—based on understanding, maturity, mental state, age, or some other cultural factor—can vary significantly between cultures. Concepts of both privacy and confidentiality vary significantly from culture to culture. Even informed consent can be difficult to accommodate when cultural values about the consent of the group take precedence over the consent of the individual. Ethnographic research often requires the informed consent of a community prior to having the opportunity to secure informed consent from individual participants.

## Thought Questions

1. How does the basic definition of respect for persons differ across major cultural boundaries?

2. At least part of the definition of respect for persons in The Belmont Report and in various international ethical guidelines is heavily influenced by Western philosophy and by religious precepts (Christianity, Islam, Judaism) with regard to autonomy and free will. Cultures vary significantly in terms of defining and expressing of both autonomy and free will.

    - How does the concept of individually based "informed consent" potentially violate the principle of cultural relativism (following the local cultural rules) in some cultures?
    - How can that process be accommodated when the local rules state that women, or the elderly, or other individuals do not have free will?

3. How can one meet the requirements of informed consent for individuals when a community or culture refuses to recognize the rights of certain individuals to give consent?

4. How do crosscultural differences in the definitions of privacy and confidentiality change the promises that researchers need to make to research participants?

5. As a linguistic anthropologist you recognize the importance of words as being symbols as well as tools of communication. How would you decide whose words/vocabulary to employ in the discus-

sions among doctors, nurses, and patients? Remember that their words—and your control of them—reflect your ability to assist them with their communication.

6. You are a biological anthropologist hired to facilitate better communication and understanding of medical procedures in a country that is not your own. You understand the biological consequences of the proposed procedures, and you understand the physical reasons why they might be necessary. Whose explanatory framework do you employ in discussing these procedures and their consequences in a group with the doctors, nurses, and patients, and why?

## Ethical Dilemma:
## Voluntary Participation in Clinical Trials

Anthropological research is often conducted in alliance with practitioners from education, agriculture, medicine, development, community leadership, political movements, and other professional groups, and it frequently occurs in international settings. Regardless of where and with whom the research and/or practice takes place, the cultural context is critical to consider. But when crossing cultural boundaries, the application of ethical guidelines must take into account both the cultural rules of the receiver and the sender countries. The question that then arises is, how can various and distinct, and perhaps conflicting views be respected? Two tenets central to The Belmont Report are those of protecting vulnerable individuals and populations (beneficence) and the process of informed consent (respect for persons). Sometimes researchers and practitioners must decide what to do when these two critical principles appear to be in conflict with one another and, consequently, create an ethical dilemma for the research.

The Woodsong et al. (2006) case demonstrates the conflicts that ensued during a HIV-prevention clinical trials project outside of the U.S. in which the researchers were from the U.S., but the population sought for participation were not. In this case, the trials were to test the efficacy of a microbicides barrier to HIV transmission. The difficulty was how to recruit women into the trials and simultaneously protect their ability to give a free and informed consent to participate. This was complicated by the fact that, in this research situation, gender shaped power relations that were translated into women not being allowed to make decision by or for themselves. Male kinsmen must make those for them, thus compromising the women's autonomy, and their ability to give informed consent free from social pressure as required by professional ethics.

The researchers must struggle to resolve an ethical quandary between the appropriate level of respect for autonomy that is required in informed consent and the protection of vulnerable populations with diminished autonomy.

- How can researchers reconcile the values of Western bioethics with the values of non-Western cultural beliefs related to autonomy and informed consent (and local gender roles and decision making) in a clinical trial setting testing the efficacy of topical microbicides used to prevent HIV infection?
- What are the risks to the society of not involving spouses or partners in the informed consent process?
- What are the risks to participants if partners or spouses are involved in the informed consent process?
- How should the risks to society be weighed against the risks to individual participants?
- How does the principle of justice help resolve this issue?
- How is the principle of do no harm threatened by either including or excluding the partners?
- How can the action of informed consent be used to resolve this issue?
- Both including and excluding partners in the informed consent process could cause a threat to the actual research (and therefore the good that could be produced by the research findings). Which action most strongly threatens the validity and usefulness of the findings?
- If the World Health Organization or global health groups performing microbicide trials involve community leaders in the informed consent process, can people's right to voluntary participation in the study be protected? Could this process be considered coercion if the community leaders strongly urge people to participate or recruit participants?

### Recommended Resource Material

Blanc, A. K. 2001. The Effect of power in sexual relationships on sexual and reproductive health: An examination of evidence. *Studies in Family Planning* 32(3):189–213.

Cook, R. J. and B. M. Dickens. 1999. Ethics, justice and women's health. *International Journal of Gynecology and Obstetrics* 64(1):81–85.

Farmer, P., M. Connors, and J. Simmons (Eds.). 1996. Women, poverty and AIDS: Sex, drugs and structural violence. Monroe, ME: Common Courage Press. Sternberg, P. and J. Hubley. 2004. Evaluating men's involvement as a strategy in sexual and reproductive health promotion. *Health Promotion International* 19(3):389–396.

Woodsong, Cynthia, Kathleen MacQueen, Emily Namy, Seema Sahay, Neetha Morrar, Margaret Mlingo, and Sanjay Mehendale. 2006. Women's autonomy and informed consent in international microbicide clinical trials. *Journal of Empirical Research on Human Research Ethics* 1(3):11–26.

This case was developed based on ideas from Kate Brelsford, Rohan Jeremia, and Colin Forsyth.

*Chapter Five*

---

# Minimizing Harm and
# Maximizing Justice

---

The principle of beneficence (do no harm) obligates researchers to create procedures and research designs that allow them to accurately predict and assess the risks and benefits of their research and to be both vigilant and effective in avoiding unnecessary harm to their research participants. The actions required by the principle of benefi-cence include identifying the potential risks of the research, identify-ing the potential benefits of the research, and proceeding with the research only when there is a clear and shared judgment that the ben-efits outweigh the risks or harms.

National and international ethical guidelines identify four poten-tial stakeholder groups whose ethical considerations should be included in any risk and benefit analysis for a human research project:

**Subjects**: Researchers have an obligation to design research that minimizes the risks and that can potentially directly (as well as indirectly) benefit the individuals who are participating in the research.

**Communities**: Human research should potentially benefit more than the types of individuals who are directly or indirectly the focus of the research. Social science research normally also has the potential to provide benefits at the community level as well, and equally produces risks for those communities beyond the risk to individuals.

**Society**: Social science research often involves an assessment of both risk and benefit to society, in general. There are a number of critical human issues, such as racism or poverty that pose both benefit and harm to society in general, based on the design and the outcomes of that research.

**Science**: Human research should advance scientific knowledge. In fact, it is considered unethical to do bad science, i.e., research that has already been conducted and the results are clearly already known, or research that is methodologically or theoretically badly flawed and consequently cannot produce defensible results.

The ethical guidelines for human research establish a threshold for harm that must be addressed in order to protect people yet allow necessary research to go forward. The threshold for establishing a minimal level for potential harm is set at the everyday risks that people face in their lives. The definition of this level of harm is included in 45 CFR-46.

> (i) *Minimal risk* means that the probability and magnitude of harm or discomfort anticipated in the research are not greater in and of themselves than those ordinarily encountered in daily life or during the performance of routine physical or psychological examinations or tests. (Code of Federal Regulations. Title 45, Part 46. Revised 6/23/05, 46.102, http://www.nihtraining.com/ohsrsite/guidelines/45cfr46.html)

---

## ADDRESSING HARM

---

Both the threshold and any harm above that threshold need to be addressed in relation to three types of harm that may be present in any human research: (1) physical harm, (2) social harm, and (3) psychological harm. Researchers working in crosscultural settings may also need to assess the potential impact of spiritual harm, because many cultures do not maintain the same level of separation of church and state that is common in the United States and do not maintain the level of separation of sacred and secular that is embedded in science. The critical action in each of these areas is to identify each potential harm and then describe how it will be eliminated, how it will be minimized, or how it cannot be eliminated and is a part of the harm that research subjects should expect if they participate in the research. This information must be acknowledged as part of the informed consent process.

**Physical Harm.** The range of physical harm that is permissible under the current ethical guidelines ranges from no harm, to very slight harm (like the brief pain of an injection), to very severe harm, and even death in some circumstances.

**Social Harm.** The current regulations specifically identify research risks that would have economic consequences (reduce earning potential, cause a job loss or negative change, etc.), any that would produce social consequences (disrupt family relationships, friendships, an individual's social reputation and credibility, etc.), and any that would create some form of social stigma.

**Psychological Harm.** The risks and harms in this area range from an acknowledgement that some of the questions asked may be intimate or embarrassing (on the mild end of the harm spectrum) to procedures that may actually have some probability of causing either temporary or permanent psychological or psychiatric damage.

Consideration of the overall risks and benefits of the research to subjects, communities, society, and science can be addressed by asking and truthfully answering the questions below, in detail. The harms that are identified should include physical harm (including domestic or other forms of violence directed at the informants), legal and social harm (loss of respect, loss of job, loss of freedom), and psychological harm (embarrassment or more serous problems). The following questions are commonly used by both researchers and ethical review committees to help explore and determine both risk and risk mitigation in human research projects.

### Risk Analysis Exploratory Questions

1. What specific harms are likely to happen to the individuals who are part of the research, based on
   - the subject matter of the research,
   - the specific methods being used, and
   - the way in which the findings will be disseminated?

2. Can individuals be harmed or embarrassed by someone having the knowledge that they are participating in a research project targeted at a specific area of their culture, especially if the subject matter includes intimate or controversial areas of their lives?

3. Can individuals be harmed if the specific information they provide to researchers were to be known to other individuals? Can individuals be harmed if the information they provide is known to people in authority (supervisors, law enforcement, political leaders, etc.)?

4. Communities have reputations and images that they want to protect, and some assessment of the potential harm to the community, in terms of perpetuating stereotypes against minority communities or culturally different groups, or in terms of the general reputation of the community as a good or bad place to live needs to be acknowledged and potentially addressed by the use of standard confidentiality procedures.

   a. Can the community be harmed or embarrassed by the knowledge that the research was conducted in the community, or by the results of the research and the information it provides about the community?

   b. What specific harms might occur that would have a negative impact on the community, based on the subject matter of the research, the specific methods used, the ways the findings will be disseminated, and the likely outcomes of the research?

5. In what ways could society be harmed by the research? This question is often addressed in terms of the overall impact of the research findings on the public's values, behavior, or identity.

6. In what ways could scientific research be harmed by the research? This question is normally focused on the strength of the design of the research, the ethical conditions that are embedded in the research, and the impact the research might have on the public's view of science in general.

If the initial answer to questions 2, 3, and 4a. is yes, then the researcher has the responsibility to accomplish three things: (1) clearly identify and describe the possible risks to any of the four stakeholders, but especially to individuals and communities, as a part of the informed consent process; (2) devise procedures for minimizing the risks to the greatest extent possible; and (3) make certain that the overall benefits of the project outweigh the risks and harms for all stakeholder groups.

One example of the ways these goals can be accomplished comes from the ethnographic research that anthropologists have conducted to produce successful HIV and AIDS prevention programs for active injection-drug users and crack smokers (Trotter et al. 1996). The research protocols included blood draws (a small but present element of physical risk), interviews with the active drug users about their drug use (an illegal activity), sexual behavior (intimate and potentially socially harmful behavior), economic activities (including illegal activities), and information about such things as sharing needles, unprotected sex, HIV status, sexually transmitted infections, and other conditions in their lives that are significant public health concerns.

This is a case where simply knowing that an individual was participating in the research could identify the person as someone who was engaged in risky or potentially illegal behavior, so the project had to be constructed to provide the greatest possible protection to prevent others from knowing who was participating. It is also a project where the specific information about people's individual activities had to have the highest level of physical and electronic protection against intrusion during data collection, data analysis, and data dissemination. The protections were at the community level (working out an agreement with law enforcement and judicial systems to ignore the ongoing research and the individuals involved in that research) and at the individual level (keeping any identifying information protected and confidential; removing identifiers from quantitative data sets; using pseudonyms for individuals, neighborhoods, and communities, etc.). All of these risks and the mitigating protections were presented to the participants in the informed consent process. The primary benefits of the project were also presented, and over 800 people agreed that the benefits to the individuals, community, and society were suffi- ciently important to outweigh the risks to themselves.

## EXPLORING THE ACTIONS REQUIRED BY THE PRINCIPLE OF JUSTICE

The third founding principle for designing ethical research is the principle of justice. Justice is defined as equity and fairness in deter- mining who receives the benefits and who bears the burdens of the research. Projects must be designed so that the people who are taking the risks associated with the research are, to whatever extent possi- ble, also the people who will benefit from the research either at an individual, community, cultural, or societal level. This is an area in which a large proportion of the principles and guidelines for human research in the United States are based on the legal definitions and the protections given to citizens within the context of the primary civil rights laws. The crucial ones for the U.S. include:

- U.S. Constitution Bill of Rights (1789–1791)
- Section 1983 of the Civil Rights Act of 1871 (provides civil action for deprivation of constitutional and federal statutory rights)
- Civil Rights Act (1964)
- Title VII of the Civil Rights Act (1964) (deals with discrimina- tion due to race, color, religion, sex, or national origin)
- Privacy Act (1974)
- Americans with Disabilities Act (1990)
- HIPAA (Health Insurance Portability and Accountability Act) (1996) (Privacy Rule, 2003: regulates use and disclosure of medi- cal records or payment history)

These laws generally define individual civil rights, and they pro- vide the foundation for understanding the concept of justice in research. The principle of justice in human research ethics involves people's right to fair treatment—a concept embedded in the U.S. Con- stitution—and equitable treatment. In order to create active protec- tions in research projects, the research design must be able to define and distinguish between the concepts of *equity* and *fairness* in relation to the specific research project. For example, *Webster's* dictionary defines equity as "the state or quality of being just, impartial, fair." The concept of fairness has related definitions, from the same source. Fair- ness is "the process of being just, equitable; consistent with rules." This becomes even more complicated because the concept of social justice is parallel to, but somewhat different from, the general concept of justice.

The action portion of the principle of justice is to design human research in a way that it is fair and equitable to the individuals who are bearing the burden of the research project. This action includes the process of being able to identify which (if any) vulnerable populations might be included that would require special considerations or protections in the research design and conduct of the research. This requires understanding and describing both the inclusion and exclusion criteria for research that may constitute a threat to the principle of justice. It requires identifying any potential crosscultural conditions that may impact the principle of justice.

Here are definitions of these key terms from standard sources.

**Fairness**—in accordance with the rules or standards, legitimate, just or appropriate in the circumstances.

**Equity**—the quality of being fair and impartial: equity of treatment. (*The Oxford American College Dictionary*, 2002)

**Fair**
Function: adjective
1 : characterized by honesty and justice : free from self-interest, deception, injustice, or favoritism <a fair and impartial tribunal>
2 : reasonable as a basis for exchange <a fair wage> <a fair valuation>
3 : consistent with merit or importance <fair and just compensation for the injuries>
4 : conforming with established laws or standards : being in accordance with a person's rights under the law <fair judicial process>—fair·ly adverb—fair·ness noun (*Merriam-Webster's Dictionary of Law*, 1996)

The principle of justice also applies to assuring that there is clear and defensible fairness and equity in the selection of research subjects built into the research design. One way to accomplish this is through the process of random selection. Random selection of participants clearly meets the fairness condition by creating a situation in which everyone has an equal chance of participation. Random selection is the process of using some form of randomization, such as a random table of numbers, to select individuals from a population to participate in a research process. This technique gives everyone in the population the same chance or same lack of chance to participate. Other types of sample or participant selection, however, can also be fair and equitable; it just takes more effort than the simple mechanical one of random selection.

The general guidelines for fairness and equity provide a framework for research that meets the criteria of being just by creating general rules for including participants for which there are special protections due to their vulnerability and for requiring the inclusion of special populations that might otherwise incorrectly be left out or ignored by the research. If the research design is focused on gathering data from vulnerable populations, then it has to contain special, often additional, protections to assure that those individuals are not harmed or coerced into the research.

Groups have been discriminated against or ignored in previous research conducted in the United States, so there is a growing trend for governmental agencies and other research sponsors to require that those individuals be included in research unless there is a compelling scientific reason for their exclusion. Federally funded research in the U.S. requires the inclusion of three groups, based on law, policy, and federally mandated procedures: underserved (under-researched) ethnic and racial minorities, women, and children. The following excerpt from the NIH guidelines for inclusion of understudied populations in biomedical research provide a justice-based rationale for this policy of inclusion. (A complete copy of the updated Guidelines is available at http:// grants.nih.gov/grants/funding/women_min/guidelines_update.htm.)

III. POLICY

A. Research Involving Human Subjects

It is the policy of NIH that women and members of minority groups and their subpopulations must be included in all NIH-supported biomedical and behavioral research projects involving human subjects, unless a clear and compelling rationale and justification establishes to the satisfaction of the relevant Institute/ Center Director that inclusion is inappropriate with respect to the health of the subjects or the purpose of the research. Exclusion under other circumstances may be made by the Director, NIH, upon the recommendation of an Institute/Center Director based on a compelling rationale and justification. Cost is not an acceptable reason for exclusion except when the study would duplicate data from other sources. Women of childbearing potential should not be routinely excluded from participation in clinical research. All NIH-supported biomedical and behavioral research involving human subjects is defined as clinical research. This policy applies to research subjects of all ages.

The inclusion of women and members of minority groups and their subpopulations must be addressed in developing a research design appropriate to the scientific objectives of the study. The research plan should describe the composition of the proposed study population in terms of sex/gender and racial/ethnic group, and provide a rationale for selection of such subjects. Such a plan should contain a description of the proposed outreach programs for recruiting women and minorities as participants. (National Institutes of Health, Guidelines on the Inclusion of Women and Minorities as Subjects in Clinical Research [Updated August 2, 2000])

Ethical research can be conducted only when the design creates a fair and equitable process for the recruitment and selection of research participants, when it creates a fair and equitable exposure to both the risks and benefits of the research, and when the results of the research can be distributed to individuals, communities, and society in a fair and equitable distribution of the results and findings of the research.

Prior to selecting participants for an ethnographic study, anthropologists traditionally approach both the formal and the informal leadership of the community where they want to conduct their research. They describe their research project, goals, aims, risks, and benefits to the community leaders, and/or others who have representative status within the group, in detail and request permission to conduct research in the community from that leadership. Ethnographic research also often requires informed consent from specific institutions that are a key focus for the ethnographic research project. These may be health-care institutions, educational institutions, religious institutions, societies, clubs, organizations, or other culturally important groups within the culture. Failing to get formal permission from these types of stakeholder groups may make it impossible to conduct the ethnography, in spite of the preexisting "official" permission of the community leadership. Finally, the initial informed consent process that occurs when each cultural informant is recruited into the ethnographic research project is a critical ethical precondition for data collection and has to be very carefully scripted to provide a full and culturally competent description of the research in a way that allows anyone to decide whether or not to participate.

The entire informed consent process—speaking with leaders, institutions, groups, and potential participants—is more complicated than the individually centered informed consent discussion that is often the only part of the process in many research projects. In most ethnographic projects, the researchers are asked many times to explain why they are there, what they are really studying, who they really represent, and what they are doing. In most cases, they have to repeat both their invitation to participate and regain voluntary participation multiple times throughout the project.

## CROSSCULTURAL ISSUES

The principles of beneficence and justice often need special attention and accommodation in crosscultural research. There are significant crosscultural differences in the assessment and prioritization of both risks and benefits that would accrue from the research. Therefore, both the risk-benefit analysis and the procedures for mitigating those risks may have fit a dual- or multipurpose system; it may be impossible to use a one-size-fits-all approach. One example of the complexity of a culturally sensitive risk-benefit analysis can be seen in traditional anthropological studies of religion. Most research done on humans is considered to be based on approaches that are scientifically based, with religion and spirituality being outside of the general focus of investigation for most sciences. However, there is deep historical tradition in anthropology to investigate the crosscultural aspects of religion, magic, and spirituality, from both an outsider perspective and from the view within the culture being studied. This has prompted some ethicists to recommend that spiritual harm be addressed in the risk-benefit assessment of a research design for at least some human research projects, especially in terms of the informed consent process. This is a controversial stance. The assessment would need to be parallel to the other forms of harm so that any kind of potential harm to a person's spiritual well-being that may occur as a result of the actual research process could be identified and then acknowledged as a part of the informed consent process and/or mitigated or minimized if that is possible.

There are standard guidelines for identifying other types of risk, but none for establishing spiritual risk to research studies. The overall consideration of this approach, however, may be important for working with communities that are involved in sectarian conflicts, among other considerations. The processes for meeting both general and culturally specific standards are explored in detail in other sections of this book.

## DATA ACCESS, CONTROL, AND DISSEMINATION

There is an ongoing discussion within the field of anthropology over who should have access to research data and who ultimately owns that data, along with the benefits that might come from the use of that data. Some of the questions asked include: Should researchers have permanent access to the data they collect, or should there be limits on that access? Some research designs allow storage and access to the data that are unlimited by time; others have specific time points when the data will no longer be accessible (it is either returned or destroyed). Should research subjects have access to any data besides the specific data they provide (access to other people's data), and if so, how much, when, and why? Should data be made publicly accessible after a reasonable amount of time, or should access be on a proprietary or researcher-only basis? Should the community that allowed the research to be conducted own the data and control it? There are groups in the United States (including Native American groups, some religious communities, and other cultural groups) who require that the data be turned over to them and that they should determine what gets disseminated from that data (e.g., published).

Debate occurs between individual, community, and cultural property rights advocates when they discuss who should have access to and control over research data. Should other researchers, who were not part of the original research, have access to research data, and if so, who controls the access to the data? Should researchers be allowed to conduct research and analysis of data sets that were collected for one reason (with specific informed consent for that reason) when their research is for a different type of analysis than the one that people consented to? One example is people doing genetic research on blood samples that were acquired during research projects in which the consent was not specifically given for genetic research. These and other related questions are key challenges for the ethical conduct of research at this time. How far does the informed consent process for one type of data collection extend to other types of data analysis beyond the original intent?

Often in conjunction with discussions on data access and control are debates on data dissemination. Most research and ethnographic fieldwork are conducted with the idea that the scientific findings will be widely disseminated within the scientific community, to the public (for the public's long-term benefit from new knowledge), and whenever possible, to the study community itself. Normally, the expectation is that research findings will be published and made accessible. There is, however, a growing amount of proprietary research on human beings that is designed and conducted for the benefit of cultural groups, companies, or organizations who demand control over publication or demand suppression or control of research findings that they do not see as being in their best interest—for cultural or political reasons—regardless of the accuracy or importance of the research. Often there exists an economic interest in not having the data available outside of the organization.

Under current ethical guidelines, both control or suppression of findings can be supported and accommodated by the research process, but it is not always clear who should control the dissemination of research findings and how both individual and community rights should be protected when that dissemination occurs; these issues are a source of ethical discussions and conflict. The Hopi Indians of Arizona, for example, maintain a Web site that discusses past abuses of Hopi knowledge and property rights. International organizations devoted to protecting intellectual property rights (e.g., the United Nations and the World Trade Organization) can be accessed through a quick Web search. One of the best basic sources for discussion of indigenous intellectual property rights is the work edited by Tom Greaves (1994), titled *Intellectual Property Rights for Indigenous Peoples: A Sourcebook*.

## Thought Questions

1. How should culturally divergent definitions of fair and equitable be addressed in protecting humans from harm or discrimination in research?

2. One definition of fairness is treating everyone exactly the same. Another definition of fairness is treating everyone as unique individuals and therefore treating everyone according to their needs, as well as treating them according to their abilities. The principle of justice is often challenged by cultural differences in the definition of fairness and equity.

   - If individuals were being excluded from research that they wished to participate in, which definition of fairness would be best to apply to the situation?
   - What if their inclusion in the research produced incorrect results, or made the research so expensive that it could not be conducted for anyone (everyone loses)? What if their exclusion was simply a logical decision and their participation did not make sense, other than making them feel wanted?
   - What if their inclusion was a demand by their community or by a community leader, in order to provide favors to friends or family? Would it change your decision to know that the inclusion of friends or family did not have any negative impact on the research?

3. Anthropologists frequently have to grapple with issues relating to the uses to which their data are put. Use the ethical principles described in this book to justify one of the three following statements:

   - Limits to Responsibility: If anthropologists ethically collect data and write reports, they are not responsible for the use to which their data are put, regardless of who is using or misusing the data.
   - Expanded Responsibility: If anthropologists anticipate that their data could be used to harm individuals or a group, they are ethically obligated to not conduct the research in the first place.
   - Partially Expanded Responsibility: If anthropologists anticipate that their data could be used to harm individuals or a group after it has been collected (a court order to produce the data, for example), they are ethically obligated to destroy that data before it can be used, or to publicly protest its misuse.

4. Who owns the data?

5. Anthropologists legitimately and ethically work for a very wide variety of groups, institutions and organizations, including universities, community-based organizations, political organizations, corporations, state agencies and governments, and federal agencies and governments (both domestic and foreign). When they are hired, they often have to sign a document that defines at least some of the intellectual property rights for the situation they are working in (who has publication rights, who has access to the data, what can be

done with the data, patents, copyright, and limits of dissemination). Based on your understanding of the three principles of ethical research, justify the ownership of the data (primary control over access and dissemination) by (1) the anthropologist who collected and analyzed it, or (2) the community that the information was collected from, or (3) the company, government, or funding source that provided the funds to do the research, or (4) society in general (the common good, the public). Which principles could be violated if only one of these groups has exclusive control of the data?

6. Who should control the use of anthropological data?

## Ethical Dilemma: The Bío-Bío Case

Anthropologists and other social scientists often apply their research and scholarship skills by providing professional consulting services to communities, businesses, and governments. Whether within the academic world of a university or the world of private consulting organizations, anthropologists still are required to operate within the boundaries of professional ethics identified by their professional organizations such as SfAA, AAA, NAPA, SPA, or similar organizations in archaeology, linguistics, and education, among others. The case described below demonstrates complex and unanticipated consequences of following ethical guidelines.

In 1995, the International Finance Corporation (IFC) hired anthropologist Theodore Downing to conduct an external audit of the social impacts of a dam being constructed by a Chilean energy corporation, ENDESA, and funded by the IFC. After traveling to Chile and meeting with more than sixty stakeholders representing different sides of the dam development project over a period of several months, Downing submitted his report to the IFC in May 1996 (Downing 1996; Johnston and Garcia-Downing n.d.). Downing's report was critical of the dam supporters' willingness and ability to protect the affected communities from harm. Interviews and observations led Downing to conclude that the funding agency (IFC), the Chilean government, and the Chilean energy company (the primary beneficiaries of the dam) would not protect the health, lifeways, culture, and economy of the indigenous group—the Pehuenche—from irrevocable harm. Downing's report was denounced by the IFC, ENDESA, ENDESA subsidiary Pangue S.A., and the Pehuen Foundation, set up by ENDESA in consultation with the IFC (Johnston and Turner 1998).

ENDESA threatened to sue the IFC and Downing if they released the report to the Pehuenche community or to the public (Johnston and Garcia-Downing n.d.). The IFC agreed not to release the report and terminated the final phase of Downing's investigation—a reporting requirement included in Downing's contract that required disseminating findings and recommendations to Pehuenche and the broader Chilean community.

In accordance with professional ethics guidelines of both the SfAA and the AAA, Downing sought public dissemination of his findings. In December 1996, after sending numerous memos to IFC management about the violations of IFC indigenous and resettlement policies in the dam project and the need to insure that the Pehuenche were opportunely informed, Downing filed the first human-rights complaint ever made inside the World Bank Group (Downing 1996). He alleged that specific management and staff had intentionally violated the human and civil rights of the Pehuenche. When this complaint was dismissed by the IFC, Downing responded with a second human-rights complaint to the World Bank's ethics officer, alleging an IFC cover-up. When he was unable to get the IFC to release his findings and grew concerned that a subsequent decision on the development of another dam would be finalized without key information, Downing formally filed his third human-rights complaint in the fall of 1997.

On this occasion, Downing filed his complaint with the AAA Committee for Human Rights. His argument was that by withholding this crucial documentation on the functional viability of the Pehuen Foundation from the people that the foundation was supposed to serve, the IFC and ENDESA prevented the Pehuenche from making an informed decision about their future (Johnston and Garcia-Downing n.d.). To Downing, this constituted a violation of his rights and professional ethics as an anthropologist, whose participatory research methods required him to share his findings with the population he studied (Johnston and Turner 1998).

While the consequences may have been unanticipated when this case occurred, now we use this case from which to learn so that these consequences are no longer unanticipated.

- What are some of the previously "unanticipated" consequences of this case?
- Is practicing anthropology for a small nonprofit organization the same as consulting for large, global organizations like the IFC? Do the professional guidelines apply uniformly across the spectrum of employers or is it differently applied in different settings?
- How can anthropologists use their Professional Codes of Conduct to address the disparities and conflicts between their personal and professional ethical frameworks and those of the organizations or institutions that they work for or with? Can they or is that belief a myth?
- What types of ethical dilemmas does the Bío-Bío case raise?
- What are the ethical consequences of taking a particular position? How does a particular decision affect multiple interest groups, including individual stakeholders, the community, academic and governmental institutions, the discipline of anthropology, and larger society?

- How does considering Ted Downing's actions in global political and legal contexts affect your interpretation of the ethical considerations of these events?
- In your opinion, what other actions could have been taken in this situation?
- If anthropologists suspect that their research and findings will conflict with the values of the organizations that they work for, should they contract work with these organizations?
- How might they be up front about their own personal ethical obligations and what the consequences of each decision might be?

### Recommended Resource Material

American Anthropological Association. n.d. The Pehuenche, The World Bank Group and ENDESA S.A.: Violations of human rights in the Pangue and Ralco Dame Projects on the Bío-Bío River, Chile. http://www.aaanet.org/committees/cfhr/rptpehuenc.htm

Downing, Theodore E. 1996. Participatory evaluation of a Pehuenche indigenous development foundation (censored IFC report). http://teddowning.com/Publications/Executive%20Summary%20Pehuen%20Foundation%20IFC%20report%20by%20Downing.pdf

Johnston, Barbara Rose and Carmen Garcia-Downing. n.d. Hydroelectric development on the Bío-Bío River, Chile: Anthropology and Human Rights Advocacy. http://www.idrc.ca/fr/ev-64533-201-1-DO_TOPIC.html

Johnston, Barbara Rose, and Terence Turner. 1998. Censorship, denial of informed participation and human rights abuses associated with dam development in Chile. *Professional Ethics Report* 11(2). http://www.aaas.org/spp/sfrl/per/per13.htm

### IFC/World Bank

Cernea, M. 2001. Risks assessment and management in involuntary resettlement. Paper delivered to Asia and Pacific Forum on Poverty, held at the Asian Development Bank, Manila, February 5–9. http://www.adb.org/poverty/forum/pdf/Cernea.pdf

### Pehuenche

Cabot, Penny. 1997. Requiem for the Biobio–Pehuenche people of southern Chile protest at the fate of one of the last great free-flowing rivers of the world, *New Internationalist,* March. http://www.findarticles.com/p/articles/mi_m0JQP/is_288/ai_30492345

Downing, Theodore and Carmen Garcia-Downing. 2001. What's going to happen to my people? *Cultural Survival Quarterly,* Fall.

This case was developed based on ideas from Kate Brelsford, Jason Simms, and A. J. Faas.

*Chapter Six*

# Vulnerable Populations

Anthropologists have a special interest in and a special relationship with vulnerable populations; this interest grew from the earliest focus in anthropology, which was on the physical, linguistic, and social evolution of human cultures. The beginning stages of anthropological theory drew researchers from more technologically developed cultures to explore prehistoric groups and technologically less-developed societies, including hunter and gatherer groups, small-scale horticultural societies, and pastoralist groups. The primary rationale for studying these groups was that they represented either an earlier stage in the evolution of complex societies or they fell somewhere on a broad spectrum of simple-to-complex cultural and technological organization, therefore providing scientists with a better way of understanding both the history and the potential future of human cultural evolution.

In the process of studying these cultures, anthropologists learned a great deal about culture change and the real (as opposed to the assumed) complexity of all cultures. Early on, the issue of vulnerability was primarily viewed on an individual cultural level, and many anthropologists became concerned over the disappearance of individual languages, lifestyles, and whole cultures due to the colonial expansion of technologically advanced societies and to the diffusion of cultural values and processes on a global level (globalization). Many of those concerns continue to persist in anthropology, but the issues of dealing with vulnerable populations has expanded to include concerns over the conditions that directly impact vulnerable populations (ethnic and cultural minority status, class-based power differentials, gender divisions, age discrimination, religious discrimination, etc.). It has also been expanded to include research on vulnerable populations in the developed world as well as in the rest of the world. Many anthropologists conduct long-term ethnographic research that takes them beyond significant crosscultural boundaries while simultaneously conducting research within their own cultures. The idea of studying others to learn more about yourself, and studying your own culture to learn more about others, has given some anthropologists a significant advantage in understanding vulnerable populations within their own culture of origin as well as within their culture or cultures of adoption. This crosscultural perspective is both a strength and a challenge for conducting ethical research on vulnerable populations.

## THE NEED FOR SPECIAL PROTECTIONS

All of the research ethics crises in the past have pointed to the need for special protections for members of society who have a difficult time protecting themselves. One of the important conditions embedded in the basic principles (respect for persons, beneficence, justice) for the ethical treatment of research subjects (and all people) is that the principles and procedures absolutely must give special protection to vulnerable populations and individuals.

The belief that some individuals have diminished capacity to protect themselves (for whatever cultural reason) and, therefore, need special or extraordinary protection, is found in all cultures. There is considerable crosscultural variability both within and between cultures on the definition of vulnerability. As a consequence, U.S. laws and guidelines and international ethical guidelines have begun to define especially vulnerable populations and then describe the processes and procedures that are necessary to insure their protection. The general protective formula for ethical research on vulnerable populations is straightforward: vulnerable individuals and populations require special attention and must be given additional protections beyond the standard protections of informed consent, voluntary participation, and equal treatment.

There is both agreement and cultural divergence on the definition of who is eligible for special protection as a vulnerable individual or member of a vulnerable population. The primary crosscultural differences in the interpretation and the active protection of specific vulnerable populations is caused by significant differences in the definition of who is vulnerable and for what reason or reasons they must be given special protections (Soskolne 1997); however, some of the broad categories of vulnerability have strong crosscultural consensus even though they do not have unanimity.

Age is one crosscultural condition that produces vulnerability. Most cultures recognize the special needs for protecting children (cf.

Freedman et al. 1993; Leikin 1993). Most cultures identify the very young and the very old as people who may need special protections, either because of power differentials, definitions of competence, or differences in legal status within their society.

> Just as ethnographers have had to tackle the implications of crossing gender, ethnicity and social class boundaries in research, so do researchers need to reconsider social constructions of children as naturally disempowered and subordinate. The issue of age-based subordination of children in research, critically examined, opens up new vistas of generational distinctions and relations. Playing with and working through the implications of this view are essential to a fully child-centered framework. (Duque-Parmo et al. 2007:5)

Most cultures also define individuals who have been institutionalized—hospitalized, jailed, housed in an assisted-living environment—as being especially vulnerable and having a diminished capacity to protect themselves from coercion or harm (Breed 1998).

Power and authority differentials and the lack or loss of autonomy are all conditions that produce vulnerability in individuals and groups (Kaufert and Putsch 1997). Consequently, some cultures define vulnerability on the basis of socioeconomic status, status and role differentials, race, and ethnic or cultural background (El-Sadr and Capps 1992). Others define vulnerability in relation to familial authority and other types of power differentials (Dula 1997; Nagengast 1997; Williams 1994). These latter definitions often include women as a protected category (cf. Woodsong et al. 2006). Individuals who are engaged in culturally defined illegal activities such as drug abuse or illegal migration are also considered vulnerable populations (Fitzgerald and Hamilton 1995; Singer et al. 1999).

The other common cultural category or condition that produces vulnerability is culturally ascribed differences in physical and mental capacity (DeRenzo 1997; Dresser 1996). If individuals have less physical ability to protect themselves, or have diminished mental ability to recognize the need to protect themselves, then their culture may define them as vulnerable individuals or populations who require protections. Reduced capacity to make one's own decisions often places the authority and or the burden for making a decision about research participation in the hands of a surrogate or alternate decision maker for the individual, with potentially harmful consequences to the individual (Haimowitz, Delano, and Oldham 1997). In some special cases, there are also guidelines for adults who do not have the capacity for making decisions and there is no surrogate available (Wendler and Prasad 2001).

Embedded in all of these definitions and their accompanying protections is the concept of a cultural norm compared with a threshold point at which an individual's condition or status significantly deviates from the "average person." The ideal is that the average person can protect him- or herself and make an appropriate decision to participate in a research project if he or she is given the correct information about the project, not coerced, and treated fairly and equitably. The "vulnerable" person is therefore one who, for any of the reasons above, has a culturally defined "diminished ability" to understand the information he or she is being given, is especially vulnerable to coercion, does not have the opportunity to make decisions for him- or herself for some reason, or is automatically treated unfairly or inequitably by other members of society.

Anthropologists who are conducting research in the United States (or research funded through the U.S. government) are required to follow the U.S. cultural definitions of vulnerability when they plan, design, and execute research. For research outside the United States, they also may be required to accommodate their research to adhere to the definitions of vulnerability in their host country or host community. The U.S. federal regulations generally define vulnerable populations as "those people who do not have the ability or capacity to freely choose to participate in the proposed research" because of a diminished ability to exercise free will and individual autonomy. The groups that are most commonly recognized as vulnerable groups in the United States includes ethnic and racial minorities, children, persons with mental problems or diminished mental capacity, persons with disabilities, prisoners, persons who are legally declared "incompetent," the poor, persons with limited education, and the elderly.

Special circumstances, however, can expand or contract the specific groups that are considered vulnerable to ethical lapses by researchers, so many of the conditions that lead to vulnerability are defined specifically for the United States in federal, state, and local research laws, regulations, and policies. For example, most of the rules and regulations for protecting women, minorities, and the elderly are defined and regulated at the federal level, while most of the specific conditions that apply to children are defined and regulated at the state level. To conduct research on children (usually defined as individuals under 18 years of age, but for the federal government it is individuals under 21 years of age), a researcher much be able to address the child protection laws and regulations of the specific state(s) where the research is being conducted. If the project crosses state boundaries, guidelines and law can conflict. The following list provides a quick resource guide for references and definitions of vulnerable populations at the federal level.

### U.S. Federal Regulations and Definitions of Vulnerable Populations

- 45 CFR-46, subpart D Additional Protections for Children Involved as Subjects in Research (text)

- 45 CFR-46, subpart B, Additional Protections Pertaining to Research, Development, and Related Activities Involving Fetuses, Pregnant Women, and Human In Vitro Fertilization (text)
- 45 CFR-46, subpart C, Additional Protections for Research with Prisoners as Subjects (Code of Federal Regulations at http://www.hhs.gov/ohrp/humansubjects/guidance/45cfr46.htm)

The general research guidelines in the United States acknowledge that some individuals may have difficulty understanding the complexities of agreeing to participate in research activities, but there is a lack of clear definition of the conditions that lead to individuals and groups being especially vulnerable to ethical breaches in research protocols. The Office of Extramural Research at the National Institutes of Health has tried to provide some guidance to researchers in this area, but the gist of that guidance is that researchers should take special care to create protocols that can be understood, and IRBs should take special care in using their judgment about whether the standard protections for a project are adequate:

> Unlike research involving children, prisoners, pregnant women, and fetuses, no additional Department of Health and Human Services (DHHS) regulations specifically govern research involving persons who are cognitively impaired. While limited decision making capacity should not prevent participation in research, it is important to keep in mind that additional scrutiny by IRBs and researchers is warranted for research involving this population.
>
> In conclusion, in all human research, varied degrees of research risk and decisional impairment call for varied levels of scrutiny and safeguards; additional protections (e.g., involvement of family surrogates where State or other applicable law permits and independent monitoring) may be highly advisable in certain circumstances. But treating all individuals who have cognitive deficits as incapable of understanding research is inaccurate and disrespectful of their autonomy. Many individuals, adequately informed, may be willing to undertake certain risks so that they, or others, may benefit in the future. Researchers and IRBs must strive for a balance that maximizes potential benefits and opportunities, recognizes and extends individual autonomy, and minimizes risks associated with scientific inquiry. (Research Involving Individuals with Questionable Capacity to Consent: Points to Consider [March 11, 1999] U.S. Department of Health and Human Services at http://grants.nih.gov/grants/policy/questionablecapacity.htm).

Most anthropologists work in international crosscultural settings at some time during their career. During that time period, they are subject to the laws and ethical guidelines of the host country and community that they are studying; therefore, they have to deal with both the international and the local definitions of vulnerable populations. The international guidelines tend to be inclusive, and sometimes contradictory, in terms of listing individuals or vulnerable populations because of the wide diversity of cultural definitions of vulnerability. The local definitions are likely to be much more specific but also might be in conflict with U.S. definitions of vulnerability due to the very same cultural differences that the anthropologist is there to study. The most common vulnerable populations that are internationally acknowledged are children, resource-poor individuals and communities, women, victims of war and violence, victims of cultural and social discrimination, and prisoners. In many cases, researchers are simply referred to the United Nations' Declaration of Universal Human Rights as well as to the various treaties and policies on human rights (war, torture, legal status, etc.) rather than to definitions of specific populations.

## THE COMMUNITY AS A VULNERABLE POPULATION

The potential for crosscultural disagreement on the need to address the varied listing of vulnerable populations is very high; the conventional process is to address local cultural definitions and cultural processes targeted at vulnerable individuals while also attempting to address the universal issues and principles of any crosscultural research situation. There is a significant need, however, to look beyond the individual when addressing the ethical issue of vulnerable populations. Anthropologists and other social scientists work in communities that are highly vulnerable to coercion and deliberate harm that extends to the entire population. Communities, not just individuals, can be vulnerable to coercion, loss of reputation, injustice, social harm from lack of confidentiality, and all of the other conditions discussed in this book.

> Investigators in population-based studies confront unique ethical challenges due to the community context of their research, their methods of inquiry, and the implications of their findings for social groups. Issues surrounding requirements for informed consent, the protection of privacy and confidentiality, and relationships between investigators and participants take on greater complexity and have significance beyond the individual research subject. . . . We argue that ethically responsible population-based studies must seriously consider community needs and priorities and that researchers should work collaboratively with local populations to implement study goals. Strategies that promote respect for populations in community-based studies . . . include community participation in research development, implementation and interpretation; adequate provision of information about study objectives to community members; and systematic feedback of study results. (Marshall and Rotimi 2001:241)

The result of treating communities as vulnerable populations requires a more complex but a potentially more ethically sound approach to crosscultural research. We have structured the discussions that follow to address both the individual and the community-level concerns about vulnerability.

## ADVOCACY AND VULNERABLE POPULATIONS

Ethnographic research is almost always directed at the investigation of the important parameters of everyday life as well as at the critical cultural processes necessary for existence, survival, and cultural comfort. Throughout the history of anthropology, much of the formal ethnographic effort has been conducted on vulnerable populations, or vulnerable groups within cultural populations, even though there have also been consistent calls for "studying up" the power and prestige hierarchies in all cultures. The American Anthropological Association Code of Professional Responsibility takes special note of this trend in anthropology and ethnographic research: .

> In research, anthropologists' paramount responsibility is to those they study. When there is a conflict of interest, these individuals must come first. Anthropologists must do everything in their power to protect the physical, social, and psychological welfare and to honor the dignity and privacy of those studied. (American Anthropological Association 1986)

This statement has sparked a debate within the discipline involving the emphasis that should be placed on the needs of some or all of the stakeholder groups that anthropologists have some responsibility to or some responsibility for appropriately "representing" in their research and professional efforts. This then causes debates over the practice of advocacy for any or all of those stakeholder groups (individuals, communities, cultures, research sponsors, anthropology as a profession, and science in general) in both professional ethics and in professional practice. One side of the debate is supported by those who interpret this statement as essentially requiring that anthropologists engage in advocacy for the people they study as a part of their overall professional responsibilities:

> Anthropologists who research and study people suffering human rights abuses and forms of social injustice have an ethical obligation to seek ways to improve these conditions. And as a humanistic field, the discipline of anthropology has an obligation to promote social justice. Unlike Anthropologists who research subjects of equal or higher prestige or socioeconomic status, anthropologists

who work with vulnerable indigenous and other marginal communities have a special responsibility to engage in support of these
groups, or advocate on their behalf. (Graham 2006:4)

The other side of the debate is supported by those who feel that advocacy is a legitimate moral choice for individual anthropologists but
should not be universally required of all anthropologists in all
research situations.

> In 1996, as a member of the commission that drafted the present
> AAA Code of Ethics, I collaborated in crafting the language that
> "anthropologists may choose to move beyond disseminating
> research results to a position of advocacy. This is an individual
> decision, but not an ethical responsibility" (CoE, III.C.2). Although
> the world of politics and research has changed in some fundamen-
> tal ways, I continue to hold this view. However, today I would add
> that while advocacy may not be a professional ethical responsibili-
> ty, it is a moral responsibility that anthropologists can choose to
> exercise if they are so moved. Recalling that the Code of Ethics is
> an educational and not a legislative document, advocacy as a mor-
> al responsibility can only be suggested as a course of action appro-
> priate to anthropological practice. Advocacy as a professional
> choice is necessarily limited to issues arising from anthropological
> research, not from those that bear upon the lives of anthropolo-
> gists as citizens, as religious practitioners, or any other non-pro-
> fessional role they may fill. (Fluehr-Lobban 2006a:5)

This position takes into account the contextual cultural conditions that frame some forms of anthropological research. These
include the condition that not all groups desire advocacy and some
even resent or oppose it. It also includes the condition that, for some
groups, the imposition of advocacy may be an imposition of ethnocentrism on the part of the researcher. In some cases, advocacy devolves
into the imposition of the researcher's moral values rather than advocacy for the stakeholders' values and position. It is also clear from the
substance of the discussions from each side of this ethical "coin" that
the right of anthropologists to engage in advocacy for the people they
study—whether they are vulnerable or elite populations—is clearly
supported by the statements on professional responsibilities and the
ethical guidelines of all of the anthropological associations that have
formal ethical guidelines.

## Thought Questions

1. What would be an appropriate crosscultural definition of vulnerability that allows researchers to understand who should be included
   as a vulnerable population and therefore receive special protections
   and special invitations for inclusion or exclusion from their
   research activities?

2. Virtually all cultures recognize some groups within the culture as having special needs or special vulnerabilities, therefore needing "rules" for some type of accommodation that would not be given to any other member of the culture.

- How can those vulnerable populations be defined in a way that addresses the significant crosscultural variability in who gets defined as vulnerable, given the culture-bound basis for that cultural definition (age, power, socioeconomic status, physical and mental capacity and functioning, privilege, prestige, status, occupation, etc.)?
- Who should have the cultural authority to decide who is included and who is excluded from being labeled a vulnerable population?
- What criteria would you use to create a hierarchy of vulnerability, so that it would be possible for researchers to make the best judgments possible in terms of who should be protected first, who should be protected second, and so on?

3. Which vulnerable populations listed by the United Nations should be added to the list of vulnerable populations that are given special protections by the U.S. government regulations on protecting human subjects?

# Chapter Seven

# Anthropological Ethical Problem-Solving Guide

It is important for anthropologists to have a competent working knowledge of national-level and international-level ethical principles, routines, and practices. There are severe consequences for both the researcher and for the people participating in the research when anthropologists conduct studies that do not meet either the principles or the required actions of ethical research. Some of the ethical lapses are deliberate; individuals may egotistically or philosophically oppose some of the existing research ethics standards and processes. Most of the ethical crises that anthropologists encounter, however, are unplanned, unanticipated, and revolve around conflicts between ethical principles rather than violation of them. These ethical challenges cannot always be resolved if anthropologists follow simple, formulaic, rules-based, mechanistic approaches to resolving ethical dilemmas in research—especially if they try to do so without taking the context and cultural conditions into account.

The preceding chapters dealt with the principles, rules, regulations, and debates about ethical standards for anthropological research. This chapter features a model that allows anthropologists to anticipate many of the most common problems that may occur in their research, even before their research begins. It also allows for anthropologists to address the unanticipated problems they encounter by being true to both the accepted ethical principles and the cultural context within which those principles have to be applied.

The ethical problem-solving guide presented in this section of the book is a systematic, step-by-step process for creating a culturally defensible solution to ethical problems encountered in anthropological

**97**

research. It involves six steps, each of which require an in-depth investigation and description of an individual case or project in order to produce an appropriate ethical outcome for a problem, or to produce an ethical research design that is intended to prevent anticipated problems.

## STEPS FOR USING THE
## ETHICAL PROBLEM-SOLVING GUIDE

The ethical problem-solving process is designed to allow the researcher (or an ethics review panel) to explore the issues involved in a particular case and devise a solution that does the least amount of harm to everyone concerned. The steps are: (1) determine the facts of the research case, (2) identify the values at risk, (3) describe the primary ethical dilemma, (4) determine possible courses of action, (5) chose one course of action, and (6) defend your course of action.

***Step 1: Determine the facts of the research case.*** In this step, your obligation is to create a neutral (nonjudgmental) and comprehensive description of all of the critical facts about the project or program that has presented an ethical problem. These facts will have both positive and negative consequences in later steps, but the basic process in this step is simply to describe them without making judgmental statements about them. Your description of the facts should include:

- *A description of all the goals and objectives of the research.* It should include the key points related to the three principles of ethical research (respect for persons, beneficence, and justice). It should also include information on recruitment processes (who is recruited and how they are recruited), on the informed consent process, on protection of data during and after the research and protections for confidentiality in the dissemination of data, and on all of the promises made to any of the key stakeholder groups during the recruitment and informed consent process, or afterwards.
- *A description of the research setting: place, community, culture.* This section describes the important social, geographical, and cultural context of the project, including environmental conditions that may have an impact on the ethics of the situation.
- *A description of the research subjects.* It is very important to identify all of the key characteristics of the population and to identify any vulnerability or special conditions that apply to the population. All of the recruitment processes and considerations, as well as inclusion and exclusion criteria, should be described.
- *A description of the research methods.* The step-by-step methodological processes included in the research project should be described.

- *A description of the sponsors.* Both the sponsors and the research subjects have clear ethical rights and responsibilities. A description of the sponsors provides information to balance those rights and obligations. This information should include a clear description of the information that was given to the research subjects and to the sponsors.
- *A description of the researchers.* This description should provide the key information on the qualifications, roles, and responsibilities for all of the key personnel on the project, including their training and responsibilities for ethical oversight on the project. Some ethical problems occur because the individuals doing the research are not qualified for the tasks they have taken on and make serious mistakes in judgment.

This neutral project description is a very important baseline document for understanding the overall research effort, including a clear description of the information that was given to the research subjects and to the sponsors.

***Step 2: Identify the values at risk.*** The second step still requires a critically neutral and reflective approach. In this step, you identify the conditions and especially the values that drive the basic research and research participation decisions among all of the primary stakeholders. This process focuses on answering the question, What is in it for . . . [the researcher, the sponsors, the research subjects, society, etc.]? The answer to these questions should provide a clear view of the values that are at risk for each group. These value descriptions and discussions, at a minimum, should include the following sections:

- *Describe the relevant values of the investigators.* Most researchers have strong values about contributing to science, society, and advancing our general knowledge about the world. They also commonly have strong values about the importance of their work and the contributions it can make to individuals and to communities. In addition, they typically have strong personal values about honesty and the ethical treatment of humans.
- *Describe the relevant values of the research subjects.* The overall relevant individual and community values of the research subjects need to be described. This would include their views of the research and its value, their community values, and the ethical position they take in regard to the research project.
- *Describe the relevant values of the sponsors.* The values of the sponsors (the reasons they are sponsoring the research) are important to evaluating the overall dimensions of the research. These values may range from a desire to address problems for the common good (altruism) to legitimate commercial values and ideals.
- *Describe relevant community and social network values.* Communities vary greatly in terms of their values toward research,

science, and general ethics. Cultural differences are very important to describe in this context.

- *Describe relevant societal values.* The national culture has a
  stake in the ethical conduct of research. One of the common societal values that needs to be addressed is the level of importance
  given by society to solving the type of research problem that is at
  issue. Problems that have a widespread and dramatic impact on
  society may be more highly valued than problems that have a
  narrow impact. How does urgency (or lack of it) potentially
  affect the resolution of the ethical problem that has occurred?

The above descriptions should identify all of the principles for
ethical research that are held by the stakeholders and any differences
in the understanding of those principles that might be caused by the
differing value systems of the stakeholders.

**Step 3. Describe the primary ethical dilemma.** There may be
several ethical principles and ethical values that are in play in a single case. The basic purpose of this step is to describe those you consider major and then to identify (based on the values that are
threatened and on who is most vulnerable to those threats) the primary area of conflict, or conflicts. The ideal is to be able to resolve
more than one conflict in this process. This outcome is rare, but not
impossible. The key elements in this step are to:

- *Determine the principle values and principle conflicts.* The basic
  question you are trying to answer here is: Which of the ethical
  principles are at risk or are being violated for each of the different stakeholders and which values of the stakeholders create or
  support the conflict?
- *Decide which conflict of values and principles is the primary conflict.* You have to identify (and decide) which conflict between
  the ethical principles is the primary conflict in order to prioritize
  your solution or solutions. In some cases, there is more than one
  primary conflict.
- *Consider whose values are threatened.* Since stakeholders often
  value some of the principles more than others, you need to determine which principles are most strongly supported by each key
  group of stakeholders.
- *Consider who is the most vulnerable.* Addressing issues of power
  and vulnerability is one of the key processes in the ethical problem-solving process. You need to assess each of the stakeholder
  groups (research subjects, researchers, sponsors, community,
  society) for the level of vulnerability they have in terms of the
  resolution of the issues. In some cases, you may find that the
  researchers or society are in a more vulnerable position than
  other stakeholders; in other cases, it may be the research subjects or their communities. There is no automatic vulnerability
  designation for this step, even though there are standard princi-

ples about the vulnerability of specific populations. Unethical behavior can occur in any of the stakeholder groups.

Your investigation and description of the value conflicts should, at a minimum, address whether or not they are a part of the ethical problem you are addressing: respect for persons (belief in individual autonomy, free will, and self-determination), beneficence (the value of do no harm) and justice.

The assessment process should include a discussion of the way in which the ethical dilemma that is being addressed involves some or all of the three primary concepts involved in respect for persons (individual autonomy, free will, and self-determination) and how it includes threats to or interferes with the four primary active elements that are derived from these principles (voluntary participation, competence to participate, privacy and confidentiality guarantees, and all elements of the process of informed consent). You must describe any conditions that might appear to involve coercion, improper information, or breaches of confidentiality in particular. In relation to the values and principles of informed consent, you must describe any problems or deviations from the four key elements in the informed consent process: (1) consent must be voluntary, free from coercion; (2) there must be a discussion of risks and benefits involved and (3) an explanation of confidentiality and privacy maintenance; and (4) the person must understand what is being said to them.

The harm-assessment process should focus on describing how the ethical challenge that you are resolving involves either anticipated or unanticipated harm, or in some cases anticipated or unanticipated (or even uneven) benefits. The workup needs to focus on an investigation of all three of the types of harm that are built into the guidelines (physical harm, social harm, and psychological harm). In rare instances, it may also be necessary to assess a claim of supernatural or religious harm. The critical action in each of these areas is to identify each potential harm and then describe how effected or was effected by the values of all of the stakeholders.

The assessment of the values associated with justice needs to, at a minimum, focus on the fairness and equity of recruitment, the risks that participants might encounter, and the protection of vulnerable populations. One of the ways that the principle of justice is addressed is by assuring that there is clear and defensible fairness and equity in the selection of research subjects built into the research design. The assessment also needs to include information on the inclusion and/or exclusion of vulnerable populations (racial and ethnic groups, institutionalized individuals, children, women, etc.).

This step is completed when you have a description of the competing values and a description of the main conflicts between values and principles.

*Step 4: Determine possible solutions/courses of action.* This step requires ingenuity and creativity. It is a brainstorming process in which you generate a large number of possible (and in some cases improbable) solutions to the dilemma in order to make sure you do not leave out any options. This step works very effectively if you suspend judgment on the individual solutions (even allowing impossible ones to be discussed) and then home in on fact-based solutions and assess their ethical threat.

There is one potential "course of action" that should be considered for every single case. That is the decision to *do nothing*. Both the benefits of doing nothing and the problems created by doing nothing should be addressed in your set of solutions. While this solution is only rarely employed, it should *always* be considered.

The basic processes for completing this step include: (1) brainstorming—generating as many solutions as possible, (2) determining the facts—describing the values and principles that are supported or addressed in each solution, and (3) assessing threats—describing the values or principles that are threatened or opposed by each solution, and (4) deciding whether to do nothing.

The ethical problem-solving process separates out the creation of possible solutions to the ethical problem from the decision to follow one course of action. The reason this is a two-step process is because all the available literature on problem solving indicates that making value judgments about problem solutions while simultaneously trying to generate them leads to a limited set of solutions—ones that are generally not creative but are culture bound. On the other hand, a freewheeling (nonjudgmental) process of generating solutions produces both more solutions and frequently better solutions because judgment is suspended and then appropriately used to choose among the solutions for the best one in a subsequent step.

*Step 5. Choose one solution/course of action.* It is not uncommon for people to generate a long set of solutions, some of which are humorous, some of which are unethical (shoot-everyone type of solutions), some of which are automatic-pilot type of cultural solutions, and some of which are innovative and offer unexpected potential. One of the best courses of action often includes combining multiple solutions into a creative whole. The time to make judgments about the solutions is after they have all been generated and described in terms of their potential support for or challenge to the stakeholder values, not before.

The steps to follow to complete this action step include: (1) eliminate ethically unacceptable solutions, (2) determine the two or three most promising solutions, (3) identify the positive and negative aspects of the best solutions, (4) choose one solution or a combination of solutions, (5) identify the strengths of that solution in relation to the other best solutions, and (6) write a description of the positive and negative aspects and the strengths and weaknesses of your best solution.

***Step 6: Defend your solution/course of action.*** The final step in the ethical problem-solving process is to present and defend your problem solution and its potential outcomes to the key stakeholder groups that are involved in the ethical problem. There are two levels of defense that need to be described. The first is to defend the course of action in terms of the relevant principles and guidelines; the second is to defend the action in relation to your personal and professional ethics. The defense should clearly describe the primary principles that are being defended and tie that defense into the ethical code and guidelines of your profession. The following categories contain questions that are normally included in an ethical decision defense:

- **Professional ethics and values**
  — How does professional integrity apply to this case?
  — How does your proposed solution meet the needs of the values that are in conflict?

- **Personal ethics and values**
  — How does personal integrity apply to this case?
  — How does your proposed solution meet the needs of the values that are in conflict?

- **How the solutions protect or threaten values**
  — Which values are protected?
  — Which values are threatened or violated?
  — Should the final decision be determined by one dominant ethical principle or value?
  — Should as many values and principles as possible be accommodated?

- **Accommodating each stakeholder group**
  — How do you justify your decision to the research subjects?
  — How do you justify your decision to the research sponsor?
  — How do you justify your decision to the appropriate community?
  — How do you justify your decision to your professional discipline?
  — Are there any conflicts in the above justifications?

If the process takes place in a formal setting, then the final part of the process is to write an informal ethics problem-solution paper that includes a clear and detailed summary of the information, decisions, and recommendations that address all of the elements of the six steps.

---

## CASE STUDY: THE SHOOTING GALLERY

---

In this section we present a case study as one example of the ways the ethical problem-solving guide can be used to identify solutions to ethical dilemmas that need to be anticipated prior to the start of a research project. The ethical dilemma described below was presented and discussed at a meeting of the AIDS Advisory Committee of the Society for Applied Anthropology, which was sponsored by the National Institute on Drug Abuse (Singer et al. 1999). That meeting brought together drug and HIV researchers to explore the ethical conditions that might be unique for the populations they study and to provide advice on how to anticipate and prevent problems with human subject ethical issues for researchers working with these vulnerable populations.

## The Ethical Dilemma

The primary research focus for all of the participants was to investigate successful alcohol, drug abuse, HIV and AIDS prevention, and intervention programs for hard-to-reach populations. The overall exploration of ethical issues and ethical dilemmas for this kind of research is made more complicated than usual by three conditions: (1) the naturalistic and participatory nature of the ethnographic research approach to these issues, (2) the illegal and potentially lethal nature of the behaviors under observation, and (3) the fact that much of the research is supported by public funding (Singer et al.1999:198). The report provides an excellent overview of the ways in which both The Belmont Report and 45 CFR-46 principles and procedures, along with the Principles of Professional Responsibility for the American Anthropological Association, frame the ethical issues for this research group (Singer et al. 1999:203), especially in terms of responsibilities to: (1) the people studied (avoiding deception, insuring voluntary consent, protecting confidentiality, avoiding exploitation, and avoiding doing harm; (2) to the general public (contributing to the public good); (3) the discipline (protecting the discipline's reputation); (4) employers, clients, and sponsors (by being honest); and (5) governments (by being candid and setting ethical limits on acceptable assignments). The report discusses critical ethical constraints and dilemmas associated with this type of research that result from the strengths of ethnographic research methods in exploring and describing people's lives. These include:

1. ethnographers' knowledge of illegal behavior by study participants;
2. knowledge of dangerous or unhealthy behavior of study participants;
3. responsibilities that arise from working with populations that differ culturally from the dominant population;
4. ambiguous or blurred personal/professional boundaries and the potential for intimacy between researcher and study participant;
5. knowledge of highly intimate and confidential information about study participants that if disclosed could cause harm to subjects, damage their social relationships, or put them at considerable risk;

6. study participants' requests and demands for researcher participation in problematic (including illegal) behavior;
7. study participants' pressure on researchers to redirect research
project resources in ways not intended in the study design;
8. responsibilities that arise because of the frequent association
between drug abuse and violence; and
9. responsibilities that may arise because study participants may
suffer from mental health problems that limit their ability to act in
their best self-interest. (Singer et al. 1999:204–205)

Some of the specific ethical decision points identified by the
group include study-participant pressure on researchers to share, pro-
cure, or hold drugs; assisting study participants to avoid arrest; having sex with study participants; observing high-risk behavior that is
especially risky to others; and allowing participants to use the
researcher's personal spaces (car, home, office, etc.) to engage in drug
use. Each of these issues is explored in depth in terms of the personal
and professional responsibilities of the researchers, with special attention given to researchers who receive public funds. The following scenario was created to illustrate the issues involved in the condition that
researchers will definitely be observing high-risk behavior while trying simultaneously to do no harm.

## The Case Study: The Shooting Gallery[1]

An ethnographer is collecting observational data in an abandoned two-story building that is being used by the project's cultural
experts as a shooting gallery, a place where people can go to inject
drugs either individually or in groups that is basically out of sight of
the police. The researcher has prior permission and informed consent
from the individuals who control the shooting gallery and provide
some services for a price, such as selling syringes to people who need
them. There are also abandoned or hidden used syringes stashed
around the place that individuals sometimes use. The researcher has
permission and informed consent from the individuals in the shooting
gallery who are injecting drugs, who are also participants in a larger
HIV-prevention study involving injection drug users. The drug users
know why the ethnographer is there and what is being observed.

The ethnographer is observing two individuals who have pooled
their funds to purchase heroin, since neither has the full amount of
money needed for a basic purchase. In this case, the ethnographer has
knowledge about the HIV serostatus (infection status) of the two individuals. One is HIV-positive but has not told anyone other than the
researcher about this condition, and does not want anyone else to
know. The other person is HIV-negative and wants to remain that way
because of fear of AIDS and the need to take care of children. The HIV-
positive individual injects first because she contributed slightly more

money and is entitled to slightly more of the drug. She then hands the needle to the HIV-negative person who does not have a needle of his own. At this point, the researcher is confronted with a powerful desire to stop the exchange of the used needle by interfering with that exchange in some active way, especially since the project has already provided information, motivation, and training on using clean needles.

At the same time, the researcher is caught in a powerful double bind, because the HIV-positive person has been promised absolute confidently and stopping the exchange is likely to "out" that person's HIV status with horrendous consequences for both that person and for the project as a whole. The project would be in danger of losing its positive street reputation and might be shut down if people found out the researchers could not be trusted to keep people's business private.

If the researcher does anything active, the project is at risk, along with the person who has been promised confidentiality. If the researcher does nothing, then the basic principle of do no harm and the researcher's own personal values are compromised. What does the researcher need to do to be prepared to handle this situation without violating either of the two primary principles? If one principle has to be violated, which one takes precedence over the other, and why?

### Step 1: Determine the facts of the research case.

- A *description of the goals and objectives of the research*. The basic goals for the research described above are to identify and describe the key behaviors, beliefs, and practices of active drug users in their normal cultural settings (home, shooting galleries, drug-purchase locations, etc.) and to identify all of the risks and the potential conditions where interventions might prevent the transmission of HIV in this high-risk group.
- A *description of the research setting: place, community, culture.* The research setting includes storefront prevention offices, people's homes, street corners, abandoned buildings, shooting galleries, cars, prostitution strolls, and any other place where drug users gather and interact.
- A *description of the research subjects.* The research subjects (experts in the culture being studied) are active injection drug users who are voluntarily participating in an HIV-prevention program for active drug users, to determine the most effective means of doing HIV prevention in this population.
- A *description of the research methods.* The primary research methods are direct observation, participant observation, ethnographic interviewing (of individuals and groups), advanced ethnographic techniques, questionnaires and survey instruments, and other standard ethnographic data-collection techniques that can be carried out in the appropriate cultural context.
- A *description of the sponsors.* The primary sponsor (funding) is the U.S. National Institutes of Health, National Institute on

Drug Abuse HIV-prevention program. The secondary sponsors are a community-based organization that has been successfully helping people in the community for many years, as well as a local university.

- *A description of the researchers.* The researchers include PhD- and MA-level anthropologists and other social scientists with formal training in ethnographic research methods, plus experience in working with drug-using groups, hidden populations, and especially with cultural and racial minority populations in the United States. In addition, the projects normally employ community members as outreach workers (former drug addicts, HIV-prevention workers, health workers, etc.). Each project provides basic safety and ethics training.

### Step 2: Identify the values at risk.

- *Describe the relevant values of the investigators.* The researchers are committed to conducting high-quality science that will directly contribute to improved methods and programs for reducing the risks of drug addiction and the spread of HIV. The research results could easily be threatened if the issue is not handled properly. The researchers are also committed to following all of the ethical standards and principles of professional responsibility. And they are committed to following the "principle of good reputation" (Singer et al. 1999:211) embedded in the American Anthropological Association and in federal guidelines that require researchers to conduct their research in such a way that it protects the good reputation of their discipline, science in general, the communities they study, the research sponsors, and their own institutions.

- *Describe the relevant values of the research subjects.* The research subjects expect to have their best interests taken care of in terms of what they were promised. They expect to be better able to take care of themselves, and they highly value both confidentiality and the idea that they may be able to reduce the risks in their lives.

- *Describe the relevant values of the sponsors.* The federal sponsors are committed to funding and supporting the best evidence-based solutions to public health problems and, since this is a stigmatized group, not to have to deal with political fallout from supporting research that not only is badly needed but is also seen as potentially negatively encouraging drug use by conservative policy makers and politicians. The community-based organization values the ability to directly provide services to the community. The university supports research as part of its educational mission.

- *Describe relevant community, and social network values.* In this case, the community is composed of the active drug users who are expecting, over time, to be able to make their community safer from AIDS.

- *Describe relevant societal values.* The societal values are mixed.
  On the one hand, this is an important public health issue that
  could reduce a fast-growing part of the AIDS epidemic. On the
  other hand, the research subjects are engaged in illegal and
  highly stigmatized activities.

**Step 3: Describe the primary ethical dilemma.** The primary
ethical dilemma is that almost any action the researcher might take to
stop the use of the potentially infected needle by the HIV-negative person
will very likely result in a significant breach of confidentially about the
person's HIV status. If the HIV-positive person subsequently becomes the
target of both social harm (loss of friends and family, loss of job or income,
stigmatization, etc.) and even physical harm (people may think that this
person infected them and that they should get revenge), then there are
two ethical breaches directed at that person—confidentiality and do no
harm. However, if the researcher does nothing (always an option), then
the HIV-negative person may become infected from this particular needle
exchange and have to take on all of the life consequences of that infection. Doing nothing may cause fatal harm in this case.

There are also secondary issues at play. The researchers may be
sanctioned by the community and potentially by their colleagues. The
NIDA sponsorship may be withdrawn, and the problems with the
project may spill over into a lack of ability to fund subsequent projects
that are similar. In addition, the community health organization could
lose funding as well as a very important and positive community reputation, resulting in much poorer health outcomes for the community.
Finally, in some ways, the dilemma is even more harmful to everyone
concerned because it is produced by a reasonably expected action that
has anticipated consequences and is the focus for part of the research.
Therefore, a situation like this should have been anticipated,
addressed, and prevented, rather than being dealt with on the fly.

**Step 4: Determine possible solutions/courses of action.** This
step was partially shaped by using this particular ethical dilemma as
an anticipatory exercise rather than dealing with it after the situation
occurred. The solutions that were generated were, in the end, directed
at two goals. The first goal was to provide solutions that were most
likely to prevent the problem from occurring in the first place; the second was to have a ready response available for the researcher that
best matched the values of the participants by both maintaining confidentiality and preventing harm to both participants (to the extent possible), given that both participants have the right to make the "wrong"
decision, based on the ideal of autonomy.

Among the dozens of wide-ranging courses of action discussed were:

- creating internal rules on who would and who would not have
  access to information about the clients in the study;

- creating ethics training modules for everyone in the project, setting rules about following the "do nothing" option for some research contexts;
- providing clear information in the informed consent process that the researchers would not interfere with individual activities even if there was potential harms in those activities in cases where the harm would have occurred naturally if the researchers were not present; and
- creating "scripts" that the researchers could use to intervene in a needle exchange without destroying the confidentiality of the client's serostatus, but also, to the best of their ability, to prevent harm from using an infected needle.

***Step 5: Choose one solution/course of action.*** The process of winnowing the possible solutions to the acceptable solutions was framed by several conditions that impact this ethical dilemma. First, the solution had to protect the project from being shut down. All of the stakeholders (sponsors, researchers, community advisory board, community health organization, and the drug addicts) were in agreement that the project's potential findings for the common good placed a premium on protecting the viability of the project. Second, there was a consensus among stakeholders that confidentiality was a critical principle and that violation of it would have very serious consequences for the project. This was especially true for the drug addicts (cultural experts) and the community-based organization, as well as the researchers. Finally, the researchers had the strongest adherence to the principle of do no harm through action or inaction.

This was a case in which the do-nothing option was strongly defended by several stakeholder groups based on several American pragmatism ideals. The first justification given was that the project was designed to observe real behavior in order to find ways of mitigating the harm of that behavior for the community as a whole over the long run, and that some harm might occur in order to meet that long-term goal. Interference in collecting data on potential harm—like needle sharing—by implementing some form of prevention or intervention would make the research less valuable and less accurate for the community in the long run. The second reason given was that information was available to the researchers on the level of the potential for harm from using an infected needle. Research on accidental needle sticks among health-care workers showed that the actual probability of being infected from a single needle stick was fairly low, but certainly not zero. As a consequence, the do-nothing option could be partially justified by the level of risk for infection for that single interaction. Finally, the third defense of the do-nothing position was the observation that *if the researcher had not been present to observe this particular interaction and/or if the researcher had no knowledge of the HIV status of the two people, the interaction would have taken place anyway.* It was only the researcher's presence that made it a dilemma in the first place. This was the weakest of the do-nothing arguments because the presence of the researcher in any research situation changes the rules for ethical responsibility. However, it is also a legitimate observation on the issue of research in naturalistic settings that requires discussion and debate for each project.

In the end, several solutions were combined into a policy and procedure statement for similar projects. One solution included creating rules for maintaining confidentiality on HIV status within the research and outreach group so that the researchers would not have information that would put individuals into such an ethical bind, at least based on data from the project. A second solution was to provide the researchers with sterile needles that they could provide to the "owners" of the shooting galleries, to be available to anyone who requested them. The third was to have the researchers and outreach workers carry sterile syringes and bleach and water (for cleaning needles) that could be provided to the drug users they were observing once they had observed that an exchange was about to happen. The intervention, at that point, was based on their reminding the clients about the things they had learned in the prevention part of the project as a "booster" for either cleaning needles or using sterile needles.

***Step 6: Defend your solution/course of action.*** Since there were multiple courses of action, each course was defended for each stakeholder group in terms of the ways in which that action protected confidentiality while minimizing harm. The actions were also defended in terms of the extent to which they protected the integrity of the research design and subsequent findings, protected the community and the sponsors, and preserved the potential for the project to provide the greatest common good possible for this particular situation.

Using the problem-solving process in a proactive mode provided guidance to ethnographers who need to ethically design the research project procedures and to train ethnographic researchers and outreach workers who would be contacting and conducting field-based research among active (not in treatment) injection drug users.

## Thought Questions

1. Can the ethical problem-solving guide be used to assess ethical problems or dilemmas that are not research issues?

2. Find a recent ethical dilemma that was faced by an anthropologist that was the result of something he or she was doing as a teacher, or as an applied anthropologist, or as a community advocate, or in some area of practice other than research.

   • Do the same basic principles apply to resolving the ethical dilemma?

- How does the workup guide have to be changed to provide a good model for an ethical workup of the problem?
- What do you substitute for the research design section (policy, procedures, and best practices)?
- How should contractual arrangements be included in the workup?
- Do professional ethics (such as the Code of Professional Conduct) have more or less impact on the ethical problem-solving process?
- Do other laws and regulations apply in these circumstances that do not apply in the case of research ethics?

## Ethical Dilemma: The Tungurahua Volcano

Sometimes we must make a decision at the spur of the moment and then, later, wonder if we chose the right path. In the following case, the researcher faced an ethical quandary, made a decision, took an action, and continued to wonder if the decision and action were ethically justifiable. The underlying assumptions are exposed and analyzed by using the RICE Guide.*

In 1999, a volcano in the northern part of South America rumbled into action. The Tungurahua volcano in central Ecuador was active and became more active and potentially dangerous to the inhabitants living on its flanks and in the tourist town of Baños. After months of the volcano's increasing activity, the Ecuadorian government ordered an evacuation of the town of Baños and all other communities in the area. The resulting evacuation caused real and lasting hardships on those evacuated—they lost their animals either by selling them for close to nothing or because the owners were forcibly ordered out of the area, the animals died of starvation. People were forced into shelters, homes of friends and family, rented apartments, and some were relocated to other areas. Four months later, when the community forced its return into Baños, the volcano still had not exploded. People were angry, felt cheated and betrayed by the government, some never returned, and everyone lost financially during the evacuation.

Six years later, the volcano again became very active, and again the national authorities worried that the volcano would explode, potentially killing people. However, both the local government and residents were extremely reluctant to leave, having suffered sig-

* The analysis of the case uses a guide to ethical values clarification created by Andrea Frolic, Ph.D.: The Frolic RICE model. We include this workup guide, in addition to the one that appears in main part of chapter 7, to help readers with the difficult process of planning ethical research, exploring ethical values, and making ethical decisions in research and practice. (The Frolic RICE model is used by permission. For further inquiries, please contact Andrea Frolic, Ph.D., clinical and organizational ethicist, Hamilton Health Sciences and McMaster University, Ontario: frolic@hhs.ca.)

nificantly from the previous evacuation. One of us (Whiteford) was there during the first evacuation and returned again in 2006 when, once again, the volcano was threatening destruction. She worked closely with the local and national governments, local Civil Defense and community groups, and with the Geophysical Institute that monitored the volcano. On the day that she and the research team were scheduled to go to Baños, meet with the new mayor, and try to locate people they had interviewed before, the volcano intervened. Its activity intensified with increased explosions and harmonic tremors, and families and communities were evacuated from the slopes. The mayor, however, refused to evacuate the town of Baños.

Recognizing the volatility of the volcano, and yet wanting to interview the mayor and others, the research team sought advice from their colleagues at the Geophysical Institute. They were told that no one could guarantee what the volcano would do, but it was more active than the scientists had ever seen it before. However, if the U.S. researchers wanted to go to Baños for the interviews they had scheduled, that they should take a two-way radio lent by the Geophysical Institute and be ready to leave immediately if the Geophysical radio said to. With that in mind, the U.S. researchers and radio went to Baños. When we got there and met up with our Ecuadorian colleague, the radio came to life and we were told to leave immediately. We had no transportation of our own, but had hitched a ride with someone from the Geophysical Institute who was picking up supplies in Baños. That jeep would take us out and it was waiting for us as the radio call came in. "We cannot wait even 5 minutes. Come now or stay in Baños without transportation."

At that point in time we were faced with the decision of what to do. We had to answer to our own personal moral code for whatever we did, and we had to be true to our code of professional conduct and meet the standards that were set out by the profession, especially the basic principles of respect for persons, do no harm, and justice. Some of the possible actions that we had to decide on included:

- stay and go talk to the mayor and ask him to evacuate the town;
- stay and find the people interviewed before and talk to them about evacuation;
- stay and alert the local Civil Defense to the information about the volcano;
- stay and organize an evacuation out of the city;
- stay and find the most vulnerable groups—tourists—and alert them to leave immediately; and
- leave and inform the people with us of the information we had gotten.

Value clarification based on the ethical principles of Respect for Others, Beneficence, and Justice as applied to a nonresearch but praxis situation provides an opportunity to think through a situation that might possibly occur.

- Brainstorm possible actions the researcher could have taken, including the ones provided in the case description.
- Choose a specific action scenario and defend it.
- Review the ethical principles of respect for others, beneficence, and justice.
- Clarify the values involved in the action you chose and justify it using the RICE Guide.

### The RICE Guide

Reflect: Identify your own biases
- What are your feelings about the case?
- What are the sources of your intuitions (i.e. your moral training, professional norms, personal history, social position, religious beliefs, relationship with the people involved, etc.)?
- What are the limitations on your objectivity?

Investigate: Probe the facts as presented
- What other information is relevant to the ethics of the case?
- Are other possibilities/resources available?
- Has any perspective been neglected?
- Are there unanswered questions?

Contemplate: Prioritize information and identify ethical dimensions
- What facts are particularly crucial?
- What ethical principles apply to the case?
- What values are in conflict?
- Are there underlying issues or hidden agendas?
- What social structures have contributed to this dilemma?
- What are the benefits and burdens of the available options?
- How does this case compare to others you have experienced or heard of?

Evaluate: Analyze options and justify recommendations
- What is the good act, and what makes it so?

Using the RICE Guide specifically for the Tungurahua Volcano dilemma, start by identifying the ethical dilemma: pose the dilemma as a quandary—to leave immediately or to try to organize an evacuation—and by situating yourself—who are you in the case, and what is your role?

1. **Reflect:** Identify your own values
   a. What are your gut feelings about the case?
      - To tell the people I trust (and know something about them or how they might react) the information I've been given
      - To leave in the car waiting from the Geophysical Institute
   b. What are the sources of your intuition? (i.e. moral training, professional norms, personal history, social position, religious beliefs, relationship with the people involved, etc.?)
      - Personal history, relationship with the local people, familiarity with the codes and statements of ethics of my profession

- Knowledge of the local history of evacuation and return, recognition and valuation of local agency
c. What are the limitations of your objectivity?
  - *Time:* decision had to be made in less than 5 minutes;
  - *Emotions:* fear, anxiety, concern for people in the community;
  - *Unpredictability:* no assurance that the volcano would explode;
  - *Concern for others and how the information might start a panic.*
2. **Investigate:** Probe the facts as presented
  a. What other information is relevant to the ethics of the case?
    - *Local history:* the town had been evacuated in 1999 with negative consequences for everyone involved and the volcano did not erupt;
    - *Local dynamics:* mistrust and antipathy between the Geophysical Institute, the town government, and the local population;
    - *Local politics:* new mayor with whom I have no personal contact and who was in constant contact with those monitoring the volcano.
  b. Are the possibilities/resources available?
    - *Formal evacuation:* the city had buses, warning systems, evacuation plans, shelters, and a new bridge ready for the mayor's order to evacuate.
    - *Informal evacuation:* each person trying to get out on his/her own with no established place to go or how to get there.
    - *Do nothing.* Recognize that people know what is happening and their agency (the capacity to act).
  c. Has any perspective been neglected?
    - *Geophysical Institute:* in constant contact with the local, regional, and national Civil Defense;
    - *Mayor's office:* in constant contact with the Geophysical Institute;
    - *The governor's office:* the governor came in person to the Geophysical Observatory earlier in the day and was being updated constantly;
    - *Local people*: the information had been on television and radio all day and night for the last 48 hours;
    - *Tourists*: probably the most vulnerable due to their lack of local knowledge and experience.
    - Are there unanswered questions?
      — *Will the volcano erupt today?*
      — *If the volcano does erupt, will the damage caused be on this or the other side of the volcano?*
      — *Are the buses, etc. really ready* (are there, for instance, drivers and gasoline in the buses, are the shelters stocked, etc.)?

> — *Is the Civil Defense ready* for the town of 6000 people to rush to cross the 2 narrow bridges to leave, to bring family, friends, and animals into the 1 local shelter, to frantically search the town for their children and relatives?

3. **Contemplate:** Prioritize information, identify ethical dimensions
   a. What facts are particularly crucial?
      • I have specialized information and access to a car.
      • There is no guarantee that the volcano will explode, or if it did, that the damage would occur in the town.
      • Evacuation is dangerous physically, emotionally, politically, and economically.
   b. What are the [ranked] ethical principles applied to the case?
      • *Respect for Persons* (respect their autonomy and agency);
      • *Beneficence* (minimize harm and maximize benefits);
      • *Justice* (treat people equitably to avoid exploitation of vulnerable groups).
   c. What values are in conflict?
      • My *desire for action* and to (I hope) protect people, and guilt about not doing anything when I have specialized knowledge (and an exit) are in conflict with:
      • *Fear of the consequences* for members of the community should I sound the alarm, they evacuate, and the volcano does not erupt.
   d. What are the underlying issues or hidden agendas?
      • *Power struggle* between the mayor of the town and the Geophysical Institute (the scientists want to evacuate the town, the politician does not want the chaos, fear, anger, resentment, and the political and economic costs of an evacuation);
      • *Power struggle* between the community (some of whom are afraid of the volcano), and the dependence on the economic domination of tourism industry (and the revenue lost if the tourists leave);
      • *Power struggle* between the hotel, restaurant owners (who do not want people to leave), and those not involved in tourism (who want the city to shelter and protect them).
   e. What social structures have contributed to this dilemma?
      • *Class struggle* between owners and laborers;
      • *Large reserve labor force*;
      • *Religious domination* by the Catholic church;
      • Andean traditions of *subservience to authority*.
   f. What are the benefits and burdens of the available options?
      • *To leave: benefit* is to reach safety before the bridges go out, to observe from the Geophysical Observatory and study the response to an ongoing emergency from within the structure.
      • *To leave: the burden* is that I didn't try to get people out when I had specialized information.

- *To organize an evacuation: benefits*—it would feel good; it would identify the failures of the Civil Defense Emergency Warning system; it might get people to safety.
- *To organize an evacuation: burdens*—it might cause panic, it might be a false alarm, it might cause economic losses both for the community and individuals (leave their jobs, etc.).
- *An evacuation would be a burden* in that it would exacerbate tensions between the Geophysical Institute, and the local major, community, civil defense.
- *An evacuation would be a burden* because it would close schools, people would leave their jobs to get their families ready to leave, and the Civil Defense would have to activate shelters, facilitate the hospital evacuation.
- *An evacuation would be a burden* because it would cause confusion with masses of people in the streets.
- *An evacuation would be a burden* because there would be a struggle for the limited mass transit resources.
- *An evacuation would be a burden* because the state government would challenge the failure of the mayor (local government) to act before.
- *An evacuation would be a burden* because taxis would clog the bridges as they come from other towns to get people out.

g. How does this case compare to other similar situations you have experienced or heard of?
- Having witnessed the misery of people living in shelters following the 1999 evacuation, I do not think that is a good option.
- Having studied the consequences of that evacuation, I have documented the emotional, financial, and political damage it can cause.

4. **Evaluate:** Analyze options, justify recommendations
a. What is the good act and what makes it so?
- *Respect for persons* becomes the driving principle in my ethical decision making;
- *Respect for their agency and experience and their autonomy* history, experience, and access to information;
- *Respect for the principle of beneficence*.

In the case described here, the researchers respected local agency, history, and the experience of the community and relied on the principle of respect for persons. They stayed in communication with the stakeholders and did not try to organize an evacuation.

This case was developed based on ideas from Kate Brelsford, Rohan Jeremia, and Colin Forsyth.

# Endnote

[1]This overall workup is an abbreviated summary of the discussions, brainstorming, and debates that could occur in using the problem-solving process to provide input into training and ethical expectations for ethnographers working with HIV and drugs. It is intended to be a guide for an expanded process rather than a thorough description of all of the deliberations for this exercise.

# Epilogue

We assume that most anthropologists do not do their research with harm in mind; rather sometimes people are harmed unintentionally along the way. In addition, because anthropologists often work in settings with vulnerable and marginalized populations, we recognize that special precautions must be considered to protect them.

Both within the U.S. and in other countries around the globe, anthropologists struggle to employ their own training and knowledge, while simultaneously recognizing the validity of cultural differences. For some, the concept of cultural relativism, so central to the development of the discipline, is a challenge to reconcile with a set of ethics derived from Western philosophy. We try to point out that many of the values discussed here are shared crossculturally and are present in many religions globally. It is how they are manifest and translated into action that varies the most widely.

Today we recognize that cultures are constantly changing and that they are never static, regardless of the degree of cultural contact with outside forces. And in the current times of globalization, immediate communication, trade and travel, we are more than ever before a single global world. The globalization of standards for trade and the banking industries demonstrate how intertwined the local, national, and global levels are. As ethicist Peter Singer suggests, we can no longer pretend that we are not deeply affected by what happens in other parts of the globe (2002). As the global reach of trade is extended, should we not also extend basic rights?

We believe that the concept of cultural relativism is still valid in order to understand how certain beliefs came into being, why they are maintained, and how power, culture, and history converge through them. In the body of this book, we posed questions designed to allow

**119**

anthropologists to think about and work through the tension between universalism (like the Declaration of Human Rights) and relativism as espoused in anthropology. We were also guided by a series of questions posed by Nagengast that unpack customs from the protective covering afforded by an uncritical acceptance of cultural relativism (2004). She suggests that when we encounter cultural practices that consistently disadvantage some categories of people, while providing other groups of people with advantages, we should ask the following questions:

> Whose tradition is it, and what purpose does it serve?
>
> Who benefits from invoking tradition to explain differential power distribution of both pain and resources?
>
> Who suffers, and what say, if any, do they have in the selective deploying of tradition?
>
> In whose name is the assertion that human rights are relative advanced? (Nagengast 2004:122–123)

We find these questions, along with idea of protecting human rights through the conscious incorporation of ethics in anthropological research and practice, solid guides for anthropology in the twenty-first century.

# References

Advisory Committee on Human Radiation Experiments (ACHRE). 1996. Final report. Washington, DC: US Government Printing Office. Subsequently published as: *The human radiation experiments* (New York: Oxford University Press, 1996).

Allen, Charlotte. 1997. Spies like us: When sociologists deceive their subjects. *Lingua Franca* 7(8):31–39.

Amar, Akhil Reed. 1998. *The Bill of Rights*. New Haven: Yale University Press.

*American Anthropologist*. 1948. Report, New Series, 50(2):375–404.

American Anthropological Association (AAA). 1986. Statements on Ethics. Principles of Professional Responsibility. Adopted by the Council of the American Anthropological Association May 1971 (as amended through November 1986). Electronic document, http://www.aaanet.org/stmts/ethstmnt.htm (accessed 3/13/07).

American Anthropological Association (AAA). 1990. Statements on Ethics. Principles of Professional Responsibility. Adopted by the Council of the American Anthropological Association May 1971 (as amended through October 1990).

American Anthropological Association (AAA). 1995. Commission to Review the AAA Statements on Ethics Final Report. (This Statement was submitted to the AAA Executive Board on September 16, 1995.)

American Anthropological Association (AAA). 1998. Code of Ethics. Electronic document, http://www.aaanet.org/committees/ethics/ethcode.htm (accessed 3/13/07).

American Anthropological Association (AAA). 2005. Relevant statements and codes of ethics in the history of anthropology. *Anthropology News* 46(6):42–42.

Annas, George J., and Michael A. Grodin. 1991. *The Nazi doctors and the Nuremberg Code: Human rights in human experimentation*. New York: Oxford University Press.

Bastian, Misty, and Jane Parpart (eds.). 1999. *Great ideas for teaching about Africa*. Boulder, CO: Lynne Rienner.

Belmont Report. 1979, April. Ethical principles and guidelines for the protection of human subjects of research, part B. The National Commission for the Protection of Human Subjects of Biomedical and Behavioral Research. National Institutes of Health. Available online at http://oshr.od.nih.gov/guidelines/belmont.html.

Boas, Franz. 1919. Correspondence: Scientists as spies. *The Nation* 109:729.

Boster, James. 2006. Towards IRB reform. *Anthropology News* 47(5):21–22.

Bourgois, Phillipe. 1990. Confronting anthropological ethics: Ethnographic lessons from Central America. *Journal of Peace Research* 27(1):43–54.

Bradburd, Daniel. 2006. Fuzzy boundaries and hard rules: Unfunded research and the IRB. *American Ethnologist* 33(4):492–498.

Breed, Allen. 1998. Corrections: A Victim of situational ethics. *Crime and Delinquency* 44(1):9–18.

Christakis, Nicholas A., and Morris J. Panner. 1991. Existing international guidelines for human subjects research: Some open questions. *Law Medicine and Health Care* 19(3-4):214–221.

Comitas, Lambros. 2000. Ethics in anthropology: Dilemmas and conundrums. In Ethics and anthropology: Facing future issues in human biology, globalism, and cultural property. *Annals of the New York Academy of Sciences* 925:196–210.

Council for International Organizations of Medical Sciences (CIOMS). 1993. International Ethical Guidelines for Biomedical Research Involving Human Subjects. Geneva, Switzerland: CIOMS.

Council for International Organizations of Medical Sciences (CIOMS). 2002. International Ethical Guidelines for Biomedical Research Involving Human Subjects Geneva, Switzerland: CIOMS.

DeRenzo, Evan G. 1997. Decisionally impaired persons in research: Refining the proposed refinements. *Journal of Law, Medicine & Ethics* 25(2-3):139–149.

Dresser, Rebecca. 1996. Mentally disabled research subjects: The enduring policy issues. *Journal of the American Medical Association* 276(1):67–72.

Dula, Annette. 1997. Bearing the brunt of the new regulations: Minority populations. *Hastings Center Report* 27(1):11–12.

Duque-Paramo, Maria Claudia, and Cindy Dell Clark. 2007. Beyond regulation: Ethical questions for research with children. *Anthropology News* 48(4):5.

El-Sadr, W., and L. Capps. 1992. The challenge of minority recruitment for clinical trials. *Journal of the American Medical Association* 267:954–957.

Faden, Ruth R., and Tom L. Beauchamp. 1986. *A history and theory of informed consent*. New York: Oxford University Press.

Farmer, Paul, Barbara Rylko-Bauer, and Linda Whiteford (eds.). n.d. *Health in the times of violence*. Santa Fe, NM: School for Advanced Research.

Fitzgerald, John, and Margaret Hamilton. 1995. The consequences of knowing: Ethical and legal liabilities in illicit drug research. *Social Science and Medicine* 43(11):1591–1600.

Fluehr-Lobban, Carolyn. 1991. *Ethics and the profession of anthropology*. Walnut Creek CA: Altamira Press.

Fluehr-Lobban, Carolyn. 1994. Informed consent in anthropological research: We are not exempt. *Human Organization* 53(1):1–10.

Fluehr-Lobban, Carolyn (ed.). 2003. *Ethics and the profession of anthropology*, 2nd ed. Walnut Creek, CA: Altamira Press.

Fluehr-Lobban, Carolyn. 2006a. Ethical challenges: New and old national security and the global war on terror. *Anthropology News* 47(3):5.

Fluehr-Lobban, Carolyn. 2006b. Advocacy is a moral choice of "Doing Some Good": But not a professional ethical responsibility. *Anthropology News* 47(7):5–6.

Fox, Rene C., and Judith Swazey. 1992. *Spare parts*. New York: Oxford University Press.

Frank, Gelya, Leslie J. Blackhall, Vicki Michel, Sheila T. Murphy, Stanley P. Azen, and Kyeyoung Park. 1998. A discourse of relationships in bioethics: Patient autonomy and end-of-life decision making among elderly Korean Americans. *Medical Anthropology Quarterly* 12(4):403–423.

Freedman, Benjamin, Abraham Fuks, and Charles Weijer. 1993. In loco parentis: Minimal risk as an ethical threshold for research upon children. *Hastings Center Report* 23(2):13–19.

Graham, Laura R. 2006. Anthropologists are obligated to promote human rights and social justice: Especially among vulnerable communities. *Anthropology News* 47(7):4–5.

Hacker, Barton C. 1994. *Elements of controversy: The Atomic Energy Commission and radiation safety in nuclear weapons testing, 1947–1974*. Berkeley: University of California Press.

Haimowitz, Stephan, Susan J. Delano, and John M. Oldham. 1997. Uninformed decision making: The case of surrogate research consent. *Hastings Center Report* 27(6):9–16.

Herskovits, Melville J. 1958. Some further comments on cultural relativism. *American Anthropologist* 60(2):266–273.

Irwin, Katherine. 2006. Into the dark heart of ethnography: The lived ethics and inequality of intimate field relationships. *Journal Qualitative Sociology Issue* 29(2):155–175.

Johnston, Barbara (ed.). 2007. *Half-lives and half-truths: Confronting the radioactive legacies of the cold war*. Santa Fe, NM: School for Advanced Research Press.

Katz, Jay. 1991. The consent principle of the Nuremberg Code: Its significance then and now. In *The Nazi doctors and the Nuremberg Code: Human rights in human experimentation*, ed. George J. Annas and Michael A. Grodin, pp. 227–239. New York: Oxford University Press.

Katz, Jack. 2006. Ethical escape routes for underground ethnographers. *American Ethnologist* 33(4):499–506.

Kaufert, J. M., and R. W. Putsch. 1997. Communication through interpreters in healthcare: Ethical dilemmas arising from differences in class, culture, language, and power. *Journal of Clinical Ethics* 8(1):71–87.

Kelly, Ann. 2003. Research and the subject: The practice of informed consent. *PoLAR: Political and Legal Anthropology Review* 26(2):182–195.

King, Leonard. 2004 (1910). *The Code of Hammurabi*. Whitefish, MT: Kessinger.

King, P. A. 1992. The dangers of difference. [The Legacy of the Tuskegee Syphilis Study]. *Hastings Center Report* 22(6):35–38.

Koenig, Barbara A., and Linda F. Hogle. 1995. Organ transplantation (re)examined? *Medical Anthropology Quarterly* 9(3):393–397.

Lederer, Susan E. 1995. *Subjected to science: Human experimentation in America before the Second World War.* Baltimore: The Johns Hopkins University Press.

Lederman, Rena. 2006a. IRB consent form dilemmas and the importance of local knowledge. *Anthropology News* 47(5):22–23.

Lederman, Rena. 2006b. The perils of working at home: IRB "Mission Creep" as context and content for an ethnography of disciplinary knowledges. *American Ethnologist* 33(4):482–491.

Leikin, Sanford. 1993. Minors' assent, consent, or dissent to medical research. *IRB: A Review of Human Subjects Research* 15(2):1–7.

Levine, Robert J. 1991. Informed consent: Some challenges to the universal validity of the Western model. *Law Medicine and Health Care* 19:207–213.

Lidz, C. W., A. Meisel, M. Osterweis, J. L. Holden, J. H. Marx, and M. R. Munetz. 1983. Barriers to informed consent. *Annals of Internal Medicine* 99(4):539–543.

Loue, Sana. 1995. Confidentiality. In *Legal and ethical aspects of HIV-related research*, ed. Emmanuelle E. Wollmann, pp. 79–117. New York: Plenum Press.

Macer, Darryl R. J. 1994. Bioethics for the people by the people. Ethics Institute, c/o UNESCO Bangkok, 920 Sukhumvit Rd, Prakanong, Bangkok, 10110, Thailand. http://www.eubios.info/BOOKS.htm.

Macer, Darryl. n.d. Ethics and governance in socio-cultural research regional unit for social and human sciences in Asia and the Pacific (RUSHSAP), UNESCO Bangkok, 920 Sukhumwit Road, Prakanong, Bangkok Thailand 10110. http://www.unescobkk.org/fileadmin/user_upload/hiv_aids/Documents/ Workshop_doc/Seminar_promoting/Ethics_and_Governance_in_ SocioCultural_Research.pdf (accessed 6/9/06).

Marshall, Patricia A. 1992. Research ethics in applied anthropology. *IRB: A Review of Human Subjects Research* 14(6):1–5.

Marshall, Patricia A. 2003. Human subjects protections, institutional review boards, and cultural anthropological research. *Anthropological Quarterly* 76(2):269–285.

Marshall, Patricia A. 2006. Informed consent in international health research. *Journal of Empirical Research on Human Research Ethics* 1(1):25–42.

Marshall, Patricia, and Abdallah Daar. 2000. Ethical issues in human organ replacement: A case study from India. In *Global health policy, local realities: The fallacy of the level playing field*, ed. Linda M. Whiteford and Lenore Manderson, pp. 205–230. Boulder and London: Lynne Rienner.

Marshall, Patricia A., and Charles Rotimi. 2001. Ethical challenges in community-based research. *American Journal of Medical Sciences* 322(5):241–245.

*Merriam Webster's dictionary of law.* 1996. Springfield, MA: Merriam-Webster, Inc.

Morsink, Johannes. 2000. *The Universal Declaration of Human Rights: Origins, drafting, and intent.* Philadelphia: University of Pennsylvania Press.

Muller, J. H. 1994. Anthropology, bioethics, and medicine: A provocative trilogy. *Medical Anthropology Quarterly* 8:448–467.

Nagengast, Carole. 1997. Women minorities, and indigenous peoples: Universalism and cultural relativity. *Journal of Anthropological Research* 53(3):349–369.

Nagengast, Carole. 2004. Human rights, women's rights, and the politics of cultural relativity. In *Human rights: The scholar as activist*, ed. Carole Nagengast and Carlos G. Vélez-Ibáñez. Oklahoma City: Society for Applied Anthropology.

National Committee for Ethics in Social Science Research in Health (NCESSRH). n.d. Ethical Guidelines for Social Science Research in Health. New Delhi, India. http://www.hsph.harvard.edu/bioethics/guidelines/ethical1.html (accessed 8/26/06).

*Oxford American college dictionary*. 2002. New York: G. P. Putnam's Sons, pp, 456, 483, and 724.

Penslar, Robin L. 1995. *Research ethics: Cases and materials*. Bloomington: Indiana University Press.

Petryna, Adriana. 2005. Ethical variability: Drug development and globalizing clinical trials. *American Ethnologist* 32(2):183–197.

Price, David. 2000. Anthropologists as spies. *The Nation* 271(16):24–27.

Pyburn, Anne, and Carolyn Fluehr-Lobban. 2006. Responsibilities of anthropologists: A report from the Committee on Ethics. *Anthropology News* 47(1):21–21.

Rachels, James, and Stuart Rachels. 2006. *The elements of moral philosophy*, 5th ed. New York: McGraw-Hill.

Rayner, John D. 1998. *Jewish religious law: A progressive perspective*. Oxford: Berghahn Books.

Ribeiro, Gustavo Lins. 2006. IRBs are the tip of the iceberg: State regulation, academic freedom, and methodological issues. *American Ethnologist* 33(4):529–531.

Scheper-Hughes, Nancy. 2002. Commodity fetishism in organs trafficking. In *Commodifying bodies*, ed. Nancy Scheper-Hughes and Loic Wacquant, pp. 31–62. London: Sage.

Shahak, Israel. 1995, July/August. Israel's discriminatory practices are rooted in Jewish religious law. *Hebrew Press*, 18, 119.

Sharp, Lesley. 2001. Commodified kin: Death, mourning, and competing claims on the bodies of organ donors in the Unites States. *American Anthropologist* 103(1):112–133.

Sieber, Joan. 1982. Deception in social research I: Kinds of deception and the wrongs they may involve. *IRB: Ethics and Human Research* 4(9):1–5.

Sieber, Joan. 1983. Deception in social research III: The nature and limits of debriefing. *IRB: Ethics in Human Research* 5(3):1–4.

Sieber, Joan E., Stuart Plattner, and Philip Rubin. 2002. How (not) to regulate social and behavioral research. *Professional Ethics Report* 15(2):1–4.

Singer, Merrill, Patricia Loomis Marshall, Robert T. Trotter, II, Jean J. Schensul, Margaret R. Weeks, Janie E. Simmons, and Kim E. Radda. 1999. Ethics, ethnography, drug use and AIDS: Dilemmas and standards in federally funded research. In *Integrating cultural, observational, and epidemiological approaches in the prevention of drug abuse and HIV/AIDS*, ed. Patricia Loomis Marshall, Merrill Singer, and Michael C. Clatts, pp. 198–222. USDHHS/National Institute on Drug Abuse, NIH Publication No. 99-4565.

Singer, Peter. 2002. *One world: The ethics of globalization*. London and New Haven, CT: Yale University Press.

Society for Applied Anthropology (SfAA). n.d. Guide for Professional Behavior. http://www.sfaa.org (accessed 1/20/08).

Society for Applied Anthropology (SfAA). 2007. Ethical & Professional Responsibilities. http://www.sfaa.net/sfaaethic.html (accessed 9/13/07).

Soskolne, Colin L. 1997. Ethical, social, and legal issues surrounding studies of susceptible populations and individuals. *Environmental Health Perspectives* 105(4):837–842.

Sundar, Nandini. 2006. Missing the ethical wood for the bureaucratic trees. *American Ethnologist* 33(4):535–537.

Symonides, J. 2000. *Human rights: Concept and standards*. Geneva: UNESCO.

Taylor, Janelle S. 2004. A fetish is born: Sonographers and the making of the public fetus. In *Consuming motherhood*, ed. Janelle S. Taylor, Linda L. Layne, and Danielle F. Wozniak, pp. 187–210. New Brunswick, NJ: Rutgers University Press.

Tierney, Patrick. 2000. *Darkness in El Dorado: How scientists and journalists devastated the Amazon*. New York and London: W. W. Norton.

Tober, Diane. 2002. Semen as gift, semen as goods: Reproductive workers and the market in altruism. In *Commodifying bodies*, ed. Nancy Scheper-Hughes and Loic Wacquant, pp. 137–160. London: Sage.

Trotter, Robert T., Anne M. Bowen, Julie A. Baldwin, and Laurie J. Price. 1996. The efficacy of network based HIV/AIDS risk reduction programs in mid-sized towns in the United States. *Journal of Drug Issues* 26(3):591–606.

United Nations (UN). 1948. Universal Declaration of Human Rights. Adopted and proclaimed by General Assembly resolution 217 A (III) of 10 December 1948.

Van den Hoonaard, Will C. (ed.). 2002. *Walking the tightrope: Ethical issues for qualitative researchers*. Toronto: University of Toronto Press.

Washburn, Wilcomb E. 1998. *Against the anthropological grain*. New Brunswick, NJ and London: Transaction.

Wendler Dave, and Kiran Prasad. 2001. Core safeguards for clinical research with adults who are unable to consent. *Annals of Internal Medicine* 135(7):514–523.

Whiteford, Linda. 2004. Clouds in the crystal ball: Applied anthropology in the twentieth century. *Human Organization* 63(4):400–411.

Williams, D. R. 1994. The concept of race in health services research: 1966 to 1990. *Health Services Research* 29(3):261–274.

Woodsong, Cynthia, Kathleen MacQueen, Emily Namy, Seema Sahay, Neetha Morar, Margaret Mlingo, and Sanjay Meheldale. 2006. Women's autonomy and informed consent in microbicides clinical trials. *Journal of Empirical Research on Human Research Ethics* 1(3):11–26.

Yeor, Bat, Miriam Kochan, and David Littman. 2001. *Islam and Dhimmitude: Where civilizations collide*. Madison, NJ: Fairleigh Dickinson University Press.

Zechenter, Elizabeth. 1997. In the name of culture: Cultural relativism and the abuse of the individual. *Journal of Anthropological Research* 53(3):319–347.

# Index